States of Welfare

JOAN HIGGINS

States of Welfare

A Comparative Analysis of Social Policy

St Martin's Press · New York

St. Martin's Press, Inc.,
175 Fifth Avenue,
New York, NY 10010
Printed in Great Britain
First published in the United States of America in 1981

Library of Congress Cataloging in Publication Data

Higgins, Joan.
States of welfare.
1. Welfare state. 2. Social policy. 3. Sociology
—Comparative method. I. Title.
HV40.H59 1981 361 81–51470

ISBN 0–312–75715–8 AACR2

Contents

Acknowledgements

In the years during which this book has been in production I have had cause to be grateful to a number of institutions and individuals. The American Council of Learned Societies generously awarded me a fellowship which enabled me to spend a year at Boston University, from 1977–78, where I began some of the preliminary work. Chapter 2 of the book was originally written for a Social Science Research Council workshop and I would like to thank the other participants for their observations on it, at that stage. Later, Roger Lawson, Adrian Sinfield and Gareth Thomas commented constructively upon different chapters. John Martin's contribution went beyond the call of duty (as editor of this series) in reading the various drafts of all the chapters. Without him the outcome would have been quicker, but much less satisfactory! It is particularly gratifying to be able to acknowledge my debt to John Veit Wilson who introduced me, as a student, to many of the ideas in this book, and I am grateful for his detailed comments on an earlier draft of it. I would like to record my gratitude to the Department of Sociology and Social Administration at the University of Southampton for secretarial assistance, and especially to Marjory Marjeram who typed the manuscript cheerfully and efficiently. Finally, I wish to thank the reviewer of my earlier book who concluded: 'This, then, is a valuable book which will confirm many suspicions as to the "Poverty Business" but does not assuage all doubts concerning the "Comparative Business".' He gave me a great incentive to write this book and I hope I have assuaged his doubts this time around!

Joan Higgins

In memory of K.H.

CHAPTER 1

Introduction

Those interested in comparative research in social policy are faced with a daunting series of problems. They must decide both 'what to compare' and 'how to compare' as well as gathering enough descriptive material to make comparison possible, in the first place. To take just one example, it is not practicable to analyse the difference between systems of medical care in Britain and America without some background knowledge of how the two countries perceive, and respond to, health care needs. On the other hand, faced with a mass of descriptive material, it is impossible to make sense of it without some idea of what the important and controversial issues might be. The key problem in comparative studies is that of finding the correct balance between description and analysis. The answer lies, essentially, in asking good questions. Martin Rein's maxim that 'What is needed in social policy is not so much good tools but good questions' (1970, p. x), is our starting point (although we would also argue that the good question is, itself, a valuable tool for chipping away at large masses of information). If we *can* decide upon a series of good questions in our particular area of research we can avoid superfluous description and acquire deeper understanding more quickly.

But where does one begin? If we were doing cross-national studies of health care systems, for example, would a study of different payment systems for general practitioners be a better point of departure than the size and comfort of hospital beds? Or would a study of hospital food be more revealing than research on the distribution of doctors, or methods of payment for medical care? The answer to these questions is that 'it depends'. It depends on who the researcher is, on what he/she wants to know and why, and on who (if anyone) is sponsoring him/her. Good questions, then, do not have universal application. They must be related to the aims and scope of the research, to the resources available and to the interests of the researcher.

Generally speaking, the undergraduate student, engaged in comparative study in social policy, begins by trying to acquire a 'feel' for the particular countries, policies, programmes or historical periods with which he/she is concerned. The problem for the teacher is how to convey that 'feel', and a sense of the important features of social policies without overburdening the student with endless detail. As T.H. Marshall observed:

> The educated public can never know all there is to know about a foreign culture. The task of those who set out to improve mutual understanding at this level is that of conveying the essential truth without teaching all the facts. (1963, p. 46)

Although the present work does not presume to deal in 'essential truths', Marshall's comment aptly captures the flavour of what I am trying to achieve in the pages which follow. What I am really concerned with is identifying fruitful lines of enquiry which might ultimately produce 'plausible accounts' of social policy in different societies, on a rather wide-ranging basis.

Anthony King (1973) has likened such exercises in comparative analysis, at the 'macro' level, to the drawing of sixteenth-century maps of the geography of North America — 'with the coastline and a few large islands picked out correctly, but with the details often wrong and the relationships between some of the parts distorted' (p. 291). Although this book is largely engaged in sketching what, one hopes, are relatively distinct coastlines, it is clear that questions of detail cannot be ignored and are, indeed, of great importance if an accurate map is to be drawn. Many students will need to move on from this book, therefore, to pursue, in greater depth, what Howard Glennerster (1976) has described as 'the traditional questions with which social administrators have been concerned'. In other words:

> how is the service working, who is it reaching, what are the consequences of delivering the service in one way compared to another, what differences do alternative administrative structures make, what is it like to receive the service, or be denied it, how do different participants perceive 'need', and what are the different dimensions of need, how is need translated into demand, what are the obstacles to access, what are the resource constraints and what criteria can be used to debate priorities? (p. 259)

The object of this book is to develop a framework within which such questions, and others, might be asked. There is no universally applicable formula for comparative policy analysis and there are a variety of ways, as we show in the next chapter, of approaching the subject. However, this book is written in the belief that every society which has developed, or is in the process of developing, a network of social policies faces a number of common problems. For example, it has to decide upon the appropriate 'mix' between public and private systems of welfare. It must also consider how the system of welfare will interrelate with the system of work. By considering the different — or, sometimes, similar ways in which different societies approach these questions we can begin to sense the character of their social policies.

But more than this, the book aims to show that comparative research — apart from the theoretical insights which it offers — is actually an interesting and stimulating (though sometimes frustrating) exercise in itself. At the end of the day, an author's contribution to learning is not so much to teach as to encourage others to teach themselves. Consequently, the present work is intended to be as much one of exhortation as illumination. If it persuades some of its readers that there is potential value in 'a comparative approach' to analysing social policy it will have achieved its objectives.

Comparative analysis: a method not a field

A number of writers have sought to define the boundaries of the discipline of social policy, in general, and 'comparative social policy' in particular. One of them, Howard Leichter (1979), has suggested that students of social policy are much like the four blind men who are led to an elephant. One, who is touching a leg, describes what he feels as a log; the second, touching the tail, says it is a rope he is holding; the third, touching an ear, says he feels a fan, while the fourth, touching the body, says it is a wall. Leichter continues:

> Students of public policy are much like the four blind men: each tends to examine a small part of a very large animal. The diversity of conclusions concerning the alleged primacy of social, economic and political factors in the policy process has, in large measure, been a product of the particular part of the elephant each one has examined. But the problems for the student of

> *comparative* public policy are potentially more severe than those facing the four blind men. Presumably the four — given a reasonable amount of time, the ability to move around the beast, some degree of intelligence, and the opportunity to compare their findings — would ultimately arrive at an accurate conclusion about what it was they actually felt. Consider the complexity of the problem if the four men had been presented not with one elephant but with an elephant, a giraffe, a hippopotamus, a gazelle and so on. Students of comparative public policy are like blind men in a corral of exotic animals. (pp. 8–9)

However, the prospects for ever making sense of what they touch and feel are not as gloomy as the above passage may imply. Others, after all, have been there before them. The creatures in the corral have, at least, certain features in common. While they are *unlike* each other in certain respects, they are *more like* each other than they are like different species altogether, such as birds or fish. They have sufficient identifiable characteristics for them to have been classified and named. The blind men will be able to establish that each has four legs, rather than fins or wings, so that each know he is dealing with a certain *kind* of creature. He will have some sense of whether he is dealing with a large or small creature, something which is fast moving or something which is slow, and so on. By comparing notes with his fellows, and by drawing on his prior knowledge, he may even be able to say exactly what creature he is touching. And so it is with the study of social policies. We rarely begin with a *tabula rasa* and we can almost always pick out some clues which will lead us to other clues and help us to understand what manner of beast we are dealing with.

As Sanders (1976) has observed, the techniques of the sociologist are much like those of a detective. The sociologist rarely begins with no clues at all; in his investigation — in most instances — he has some preconceptions about what is 'normal', 'reasonable' and 'predictable'. Similarly, as Sanders points out, 'the stereotype of the detective who asks for "just the facts" is inaccurate for detectives are always working with, and testing, "theory" '(p. 3). In a case of murder the detective will often begin by questioning the family and friends of the victim, because he knows that a high proportion of murderers are known to (often married to) their victims. Similarly, Sanders argues, 'sociologists develop theories that lead them to ask certain questions and not others and these questions, in turn, lead them to notice certain "facts" and not others' (p. 3). The model of the sociological detective, concerned as much with formulating questions as with finding answers, is one which we shall develop as we go along.

The object of these preliminary remarks, however, is not to develop the perfect analogy but to illustrate that what we are concerned with is not a *field* of study, but a *method* of study. It is important to establish from the outset, then, that 'comparative social policy' is not really a distinct discipline at all. In fact, the phrase is something of a misnomer. Taken literally, it is not social policies themselves which are comparative, but the *study* of them; hence we have tended to refer to comparative analysis or comparative research in social policy as being a more accurate description of the activity in which we are engaged. Furthermore, what passes for 'comparative social policy' is much more often concerned with contrasts than comparisons. However, more important than these points about terminology is the fact that there is no coherent field of study around which one can draw boundaries and declare that 'this is comparative social policy'. Indeed, a modest survey of teachers and researchers in Britain (conducted by the Joint University Council for Social and Public Administration, Comparative Social Administration Group, in 1978) shows that a very wide range of approaches is subsumed under the heading of comparative social policy and administration. There was interest not only in the countries of Europe, but also in the United States, Russia, Japan, Israel, Hong Kong, Singapore and the Third World. The particular services and issues being investigated also ranged broadly from research on day centres and child support provisions to work on the development of welfare in the British Empire and on the relationship between capitalism and welfare. However, the main factor (indeed, in some cases, the only factor) which this work had in common was the use of comparison to collect and explore the kind of data which, probably, could not be elicited by other methods. One aim of a book such as this, therefore, must be to look for a series of lowest common denominators in such a multitude of interests.

One of the advantages which comparative methods offer the sociologist or the student of social policy is that, quite often, it is the nearest he/she will get to a laboratory situation. A series of moral and practical difficulties in social research present themselves, particularly in the social welfare context. It would, for example, be very difficult to justify an experiment in which one group of the population was afforded a range of emergency medical services while a control group was denied any facilities. However, we can use comparisons with other countries (such as the United States), or other historical periods (Britain before the introduction of the National Health Service) to investigate how people may, or do actually respond to, situations in which publicly provided medical services are not freely available. We may find that they resort to private insurance schemes, or that private entrepreneurs provide facilities on a fee-for-service basis, or that non-medical facilities (such as the fire brigade or police) provide emergency care.

Similarly, the researcher may not always be in a position to collect 'before and after' data. He/she will find it difficult, therefore, to measure the outcome or effects of a particular policy initiative. For example, we may wish to know whether the introduction of free school meals and milk in Britain significantly improved the health of schoolchildren and whether it improved their concentration span during the school day. We may find that the data (if any) collected prior to the introduction of these measures was either incomplete, or of dubious validity. However, an alternative would be to look at those States of America in which free school meals and milk are not available and compare the health of schoolchildren there with that of children in Britain and in other States where they are available. Obviously we must be aware that the influence of completely extraneous factors will affect our results. Nevertheless, the use of comparisons adds a dimension to our research which might not otherwise be there, and enables us to form some impression, however imprecise, of the possible effects of introducing (or, indeed, abolishing) free school meals and milk.

'Comparative social policy', as it has come to be known, is not then a discrete area of study, separate from the main body of social policy studies, and reserved for the slightly suspect voyeur of practices in foreign lands. On the contrary, it deals with issues and uses techniques which are absolutely central to the analysis of social policy in modern industrial societies. This book is concerned not with drawing boundaries around a specific area of specialist study, but with demonstrating how the use of a comparative methodology can highlight some of the key issues in social policy in different societies. In many respects it is a book for the do-it-yourself enthusiast. It tries to show how to begin the process of using comparative data for the purpose of analysing the broad outlines of social policy both historically and cross-nationally. It gives some indication of what tools will be needed for the job and which pieces one might start fitting together.

Readers may be confused to discover that the book is not arranged in the conventional manner of textbooks on comparative social policy. In other words, it is not organized on a country by country basis, or in the form of comparing social services in different countries. It adopts a much more eclectic approach, focusing on a number of important issues in social policy and drawing upon examples from various policy areas and societies to illustrate a series of general propositions.

The art of comparing

In many respects what we are proposing here, i.e. the use of comparisons to evaluate and explain, is neither new nor unusual. On the contrary, acts of comparing are part of our daily lives. In order to make sense of the world, or in order to measure the value of different phenomena, we are constantly making comparisons. For example, parents are frequently anxious to know how their children are progressing — as babies they will compare them with other babies (or with their older brothers and sisters as the same age) to see whether they are unusually fat or thin, small or large; they will compare notes with other parents about their childrens' progress in crawling, walking, talking, and later, reading and writing. At school, teachers measure the development of children against each other, and against past performances, so that the child's work is compared with that of his/her peers and with his/her own attainment in previous years.

To take another example, a photographer will often compose a picture in such a way that those looking at it can make sense of it by comparing the familiar with the unfamiliar. So, for instance, if his subject is a mountain landscape he may place a figure in the foreground so that we get a sense of height and depth. We have some conception of the size of an average human and by comparing the figure visually with the background we get some idea of the height of the hills and the depths of the valleys. Similarly, if he is taking pictures of scientific or natural specimens, he will often photograph them against a hand or a foot, say, or against a six-inch rule. By comparing the objects which we do not recognize with the objects we are familiar with, we can get some idea of the size of the former.

Another more topical example comes from the world of industrial relations. Pay bargaining is frequently couched in terms of relativities, and comparability between different groups of workers.

Trade union negotiators do not operate with the notion of a 'fair wage' as an absolute and totally objective measure. Instead they compare the wages of their members with those of other similar groups, and with changes in the cost of living. Thus university teachers, for example, have traditionally compared themselves with civil servants and would expect (although their expectations are not always fulfilled) to maintain parity with them. Comparability studies have become an increasingly important facet of pay bargaining.

Finally, we can take an example from the field of social policy to show the different ways in which comparisons can be used for the purpose of evaluation. In November 1979, in London, a study of the maternity grant was published. It coincided with the introduction in the House of Commons of a Private Member's Bill to increase the size of the grant. In looking at the maternity grant in 1979 we may begin with the knowledge that its value was £25. However, that knowledge alone is completely meaningless because, without comparative evidence, we have no sense of its generosity or adequacy. It might be, for example, that the average industrial wage was £25 per annum, in which case the maternity grant would be extremely valuable. It might be, on the other hand, that £25 was the cost of one packet of disposable nappies, in which case it would be totally inadequate. We must, therefore, look for indices against which to measure the £25 grant to give us some idea of its real value. At the same time, these indices must be broadly relevant to the question in hand. There is not much point, for example, comparing the size of the grant with the cost of a holiday for two in Miami because, although this might give us a very vague idea of what £25 was really worth, it wouldn't tell us much about the adequacy of the £25 grant to fulfill the purposes for which it was intended.

Thus, the author of the report, without necessarily purporting to be engaged in a detailed comparative study, does suggest a series of points of comparison which help us to estimate the contemporary value and significance of a £25 maternity grant. First of all, he measures expenditure on the grant as a percentage of all social security spending. It amounts to only 0.105 per cent of the total. We can see, therefore, that — compared with other types of social security expenditure — it is a small commitment. Secondly, the author uses historical comparisons to show that the real value of the grant was actually less in 1979 than it was when first introduced in 1911. In order to reach this conclusion he used a third index of comparison which was the size of the grant compared with changing price levels (and to some extent with the 'cost of living' and the 'rate of inflation'). If the 1911 standard were to be maintained, and the grant completely 'inflation-proofed', payment in 1979 would have to be increased to £110. Thirdly, the adequacy of the grant is calculated by measuring it against the actual costs of the basic items needed for a new baby. The total cost of this 'basket of goods' in June 1979 amounted to £162.40, thus indicating that the £25 grant was far from adequate. Finally, the author compares the level of the maternity grant in Britain with that in other countries. His conclusion is that many of the European countries pay benefits at much higher levels than the British (Norway: £573; Austria: £567; France: £385). This is equally true of countries with both higher and lower Gross Domestic Products. Indeed, were it not for the ready availability of the grant in Britain (compared with its restricted coverage elsewhere) the author concludes that:

> we would find ourselves falling behind Niger, Cameroon, the Ivory Coast and Madagascar in the Social Security league tables since these countries all manage to pay maternity grants of more than £25 to the wives of those in regular paid employment. (Kendall, 1979, p. 16)

With each of these pieces of comparative knowledge superimposed upon the next, therefore, we are able to build up a picture of the value of the British £25 maternity grant in 1979. Some of the comparisons, as the author readily acknowledges, have certain limitations. However, taken together, they produce a composite picture which could not have been achieved by other means. This one case study neatly illustrates the uses and potential of different types of comparison in giving meaning to an otherwise relatively meaningless phenomenon.

As we have shown, comparisons of many different kinds are an important part of everyday life. Almost all forms of evaluation, in its most literal sense, involve an element of comparison. To suggest in this book, therefore, that we should use comparisons, in a more systematic way, to evaluate social policies should be a singularly unexceptional proposal. However, the use of comparative methods in the study of social policy is probably the most underdeveloped region of academic and empirical research. Indeed, comparative research, in some cases, has been actively opposed by those who argue that, because of the methodological problems involved, it can be positively misleading. They are, no doubt, right to caution against the dangers of comparing like with unlike, and the assumption that the outcome has some watertight validity. However, no one who compares an elephant with a mouse and finds the one to be larger than the other fails to perceive that there are other significant differences between them. Equally, researchers who use comparative data to highlight the similarities and differences between countries are usually aware that there are other elements in the comparison which may force them to qualify their conclusions. The answer is not to stop comparing elephants with mice (or social security expenditure in Britain and America) but to cultivate an awareness that there are limitations as well as advantages to such comparisons. In the illustration quoted above, for example, the author of the report on maternity grants observed that the availability of maternal health services, and the cost of maternity, in different countries had a bearing on the value of the grant. The conclusion to be drawn here, therefore, is that strict comparisons between the real value of the grant, cross-nationally, are impossible to make, but this does not invalidate the point that — generally speaking — Britain is significantly less generous in the payments it makes than many other (less advanced) countries.

In a book of this kind (designed primarily for the undergraduate student) we are attempting to do no more than to convey a very broad impression of the shape and form of social policy, and of the issues in social policy, in different countries. The dire warnings of the anti-comparativists who argue that precision is impossible are, therefore, largely irrelevant. No one should be deterred from seeking *some* answers because they fear that the ones they do find will not be perfect.

CHAPTER 2

Approaches to Comparison in Social Policy

The purpose of this chapter is to identify some of the main approaches to comparative research in social policy. Its aim is not so much to provide a comprehensive review of the literature as to illustrate how we might begin to classify those works which, however loosely, involve the use of comparison to describe and evaluate developments in social policy. It is probably true that the failure to attempt such classificatory exercises, especially in British studies of social policy, has contributed to the current paucity of theoretical work on comparative methodology within this sphere of social activity. Obviously a number of approaches to classification are possible. What follows is just one preliminary attempt to categorize what are some of the better known examples of their genre. As Eckstein and Apter observe, such a process is an important prelude to the development of more systematized and coherent theory:

> Science begins with the effort to order and classify the objects of the universe. This is first a job of comparison, but comparison is not limited to the purely classificatory. It can, and must, be used as a method for determining useful theories. (1963, p. vi)

This chapter also shows how wide has been the range of studies which contain a comparative element. Although they have a number of features in common, there is obviously no simple, unitary 'comparative method' as such. The particular approach one favours must clearly be determined by the kind of questions one is trying to answer. The chapter itself is concerned with two issues. Firstly, what are the advantages and limitations of comparative research in social policy and secondly, what form have comparative studies taken, and what have been their main characteristics?

The advantages and limitations of comparisons in social policy

The value of comparative research in social policy is not self-evident and its potential contribution needs to be examined closely. Although comparative studies have become increasingly fashionable there is no reason to believe that comparison, *per se*, is a 'good thing'. The present mood is a complete reversal of the traditional view that comparative research was so riddled with pitfalls that it was barely worth attempting. Introductions to comparative studies in social policy (for example, Briggs, 1972; Heclo, 1974; Rodgers, 1977), even while advocating a comparative approach, often contained such dire warnings about the methodological problems involved in definition and measurement that the fainthearted might have been deterred from comparative work altogether. It is important, therefore, to find a middle way, in which both the advantages and limitations of comparisons can be identified and dealt with.

Probably the most important reason for engaging in comparative research is that it encourages a distinction between the general and the specific. Rodgers *et al.* claim, for example, that:

> Comparative studies increase the student's ability to distinguish the general from the specific, if only to identify what is 'generally true' for all countries and what is unique and 'specifically true' to any situation. (1968, p. 11)

Similarly, Heclo has argued that:

> To speak of comparative analysis suggests not only that one will be looking at variables which actually vary, but also that one will be doing so in contexts which themselves vary. Even for the contemporary nominalist, it is only through such comparative analysis that one can appreciate what are the truly unique and what are the more generic phenomena. (1972, p. 95)

The validity of such an argument can be seen particularly in relation to social policy. Without some degree of comparison we are unable to say whether problems of policy are peculiar to certain types of political and economic system or whether problems are inherent in the policies themselves. Does compensatory education, for example, present the same difficulties and offer the same opportunities in different kinds of social and educational systems? Alternatively, we might ask are 'welfare states' inevitable features of industrialized societies? Many such questions can only be answered through comparative research.

Indeed, on a much broader level, evaluation and learning can *only* take place when comparisons are made. As Durkheim remarked, in his *Rules of Sociological Method:*

> Comparative sociology is not a particular branch of sociology; it is sociology itself, insofar as it ceases to be purely descriptive and aspires to account for facts. (1938, p. 139)

Radcliffe-Brown, another early proponent of comparative research, also argued that:

> It is only by the use of the comparative method that we can arrive at general explanations. The alternative is to confine ourselves to particularistic explanations, similar to those of the historian. The two kinds of explanation are both legitimate and do not conflict, but both are needed for the understanding of societies and their institutions. (1952, pp. 113–14)

Though one might question Radcliffe-Brown's notion of history, the basic point is clear. Analysis, explanation and the drawing of generalizations in the social sciences frequently necessitate the use of comparative data.

A second advantage of comparisons in social policy is that they widen our understanding of the range of policy options. In other words, if we are seeking to meet particular social needs, a knowledge of alternative courses of action is frequently helpful. Ethnocentrism limits our familiarity with different ways of solving problems and may lead to the conclusion that the present way of doing things, and *our* way of doing things, is the only way of doing them. This particular rationale for undertaking comparative studies was the one identified by Christine Cockburn and Hugh Heclo in their report on the treatment of one-parent families, which appeared as an appendix to the Finer Report:

> Nations can learn from the experience of others, and even where lessons are ambiguous, different approaches can suggest a broader range of policy options than might appear in isolation. (Finer, 1974, p. 16)

This quotation also points to another benefit of comparative studies which is that of lesson-learning. A number of these studies have set out quite explicitly to learn lessons from other countries (see, for example, Rose, 1974). This is particularly true of research orientated towards policy development. In other studies either the lessons remain implicit, or their practical applications are left implicit. During the 1960s and 1970s British and American social scientists and policy-makers were increasingly active in their attempts to learn lessons from the other's experience (although usually with little success). America looked to Britain for ideas on State-provided health care, and for lessons from the National Health Service (see Marmor and Bridges, 1977; Heidenheimer et al., 1976, chapter 1). Britain examined American experiments in compensatory education (Little and Smith, 1971; Halsey, 1972), community action, anti-poverty programmes and urban policy (Home Office, 1969; Deakin, 1974; Higgins, 1978). There are, of course, certain dangers in lesson-drawing. The lessons may be inadequately learned so that one country is lured into imitating the policies of another without sufficient regard for differences in national contexts. As Cockburn and Heclo warned:

> No foreign programme is so simple or so isolated from its national context as to commend itself for direct importation into another country. (Finer, 1974, p. 16)

The potential for learning lessons from comparative studies in social policy is considerable, but it is not without its pitfalls. 'Lesson-drawing', as Richard Rose observed, 'is a difficult art' (Rose, 1974, p. 11).

A further advantage of comparison, both historically and cross-nationally, is that we are able to identify and evaluate 'fashions' in social policy. The last 20 years have thrown up a series of, often short-lived, fashions which have significantly influenced the direction of policy in different countries. These include experiments in 'participation', 'positive discrimination', 'community action', 'compensatory education', 'action research' and 'area programmes'. Comparison allows analysis of the 'natural histories' of such concepts and enables us to predict outcomes.

Finally, the overall advantage of comparison in social policy is that it permits the researcher to identify the social determinants of policy and to differentiate between culturally specific causes, variables, institutional arrangements and outcomes and those which are characteristic of different systems and different countries.

Despite the apparent advantages of comparative studies, a number of important criticisms have been directed at them. Some of the attacks have been relatively unsophisticated, often invoking what Marmor and Bridges have described as 'the law of comparative difference'. This maintains that:

> if nations differ in any respect then they cannot learn from one another. Whenever a comparative finding is presented the criticism from this perspective is automatic. Lists of factors which differentiate the countries in question are supplied. The inference is that such differences render transplantation of lessons logically impossible. (1977, pp. 6–7)

It is clearly important to specify how and why lessons can and should be learned and it may be that, in some situations, methodological problems do make strict comparisons invalid or even impossible. The response to the adherents of the 'law of comparative difference' should probably be that comparative studies in social policy, as with other areas of social science, may help us to answer some questions but not others. What is important is to recognize the limitations of the comparative approach and to work within them.

A far more serious and penetrating criticism is that the majority of comparative studies in social policy have, in the past, lacked any notion of theory and analysis. This omission is particularly evident when one contrasts the comparative social policy literature with that of comparative politics, where a vast body of theoretical and methodological expertise has been built up over a number of years. The essential problem of comparative social policy, as Feldman sees it, is that:

> without a guiding theory explanations for policy become lists, constantly awaiting addenda, and comparative cases hover close to a line of anecdote. (1978, p. 300)

While Heclo observed that:

> the inheritance from the majority of policy case studies, on both sides of the Atlantic, is a series of isolated, episodic descriptions — particularly of legislative enactments — which are apparently thought to be of intrinsic interest. To only a very limited extent does this legacy constitute a body of scientific observations helping to discern larger patterns. (1972, p. 90)

Thus, although case studies can be interesting in themselves the possibilities of explanation, generalization and analysis are limited, unless they can be set in a conceptual and theoretical framework which permits a broader view. On their own, case studies are inevitably parochial, but the worst aspects of parochialism can be avoided if the studies are seen in terms of national, international or historical trends and pressures. A good deal of what is described as 'comparative social policy' is not, in fact, comparative at all and much of it consists of a description of policies and programmes in other countries. Marmor and Bridges contend that such description is simply the first stage of the process of explanation, and should not be seen as an end in itself.

> The description of international variation is . . . only the beginning of the learning process. Learning that something takes place abroad is, of course, an addition to knowledge but its relevance to policy learning has to be established. The importation of useful knowledge requires a prior assessment of purpose and focus. (Marmor and Bridges, 1977, p. 7)

Strenuous efforts must, therefore, be made to deal with the theoretical and methodological weakness of comparative analysis in social policy. The approach is still in its infancy and it is important that it develops with a clear focus, rather than in an *ad hoc* manner, without any sense of direction. While emphasizing the importance of theory we must also be wary of claiming too much for our conclusions. Ginsberg has, quite rightly, warned against:

> attempts to use comparative studies to formulate theories regarding the nature of society as a whole, or any claims to formulate the general laws of its evolution or development. (Quoted in Rodgers, 1977, p. 199)

It is clear that the kind of comparative studies which have been undertaken in social policy cannot attempt to reach conclusions which have the status of 'general laws' (the notion of which, in any case, seems highly suspect), nor have they aimed to do so. There are many other levels and types of investigation, however, which can be explored without purporting to establish 'laws' of social policy or of social institutions in general. In some instances the best we can hope for is to say that particular explanations are more or less appropriate in particular sets of circumstances.

Finally, Elliot Feldman has identified three further limitations which may arise when comparing social policies:

> There is ambiguity in the concept of 'policy', there is disagreement over what and how to compare, and there is the problem of competence. (1978, p. 288)

There are two particular dimensions to the problem of definitions. Firstly, there is debate about whether we should include, in our discussion of policy, both what governments *do not do* in relation to certain areas of need, as well as what they *do*. In other words, does the concept include 'non-decisions' as well as 'decisions'? When making comparisons between countries it is often easier, than in one-country studies, to identify what governments are *not doing* because we have a greater awareness of what they *could be* doing. A very important aspect of health care policy in America, for example, has been the failure to introduce a national system of health insurance for all groups. We know it is a policy option (although one which has not been adopted) because we see such schemes in operation elsewhere. We should distinguish between two 'negative' aspects of policy: first, non-decisions, in which issues are never posed for action to be taken upon them and, second, decisions *not* to act.

Secondly, there is the problem of how to deal with the fact that different countries define the boundaries of policy in different ways. Even if we restrict our definition of policy to public expenditure on social welfare it is clear that the components of such expenditure differ from one country to the next. The most obvious discrepancy is that some countries include expenditure on education whilst others do not. The work of Wilensky (1975) and Kaim-Caudle (1973) has underlined the very real difficulties involved in attempting to find precise quantitative data with which to compare public expenditure in different countries. As Wilensky remarks 'comparable data on public expenditures are as yet available for only a few countries and are, at best, shaky' (1975, p. 7). Kaim-Caudle encountered even more definitional problems in his ten-country study of social security policy. In America 'social security' was popularly used to refer to the Federal old-age, survivors, disability and health insurance programme, while in the United Kingdom 'social security' included all cash transfers to individuals, with the exception of educational grants. In New Zealand the term was used to refer to the comprehensive system of cash benefits and health services established in 1938, while in Canada, Australia and Austria it did not appear in official statistics at all (Kaim-Caudle, 1973, pp. 6–7).

At an even more general level the word 'welfare' has very different meanings. In America, for example, it often refers quite specifically to public assistance payments, whereas in Britain it is used much more as a generic term for a wide range of activities in the areas of health, social services and income maintenance. (It is also well known that the apparently simple description of 'public schools' has exactly opposite meanings in Britain and America.) The broad notion of 'social policy' has many different meanings, both cross-nationally, within countries and over time. An example is provided in the work of the German economist Otto von Zwiedineck-Sudenhorst who wrote, in 1911, that 'Social policy is a policy which aims at securing the continued attainment of the ends of society' and that 'social policy . . . is the embodiment of all measures which pertain to the attenuation of class antagonisms' (quoted in Cahnman and Schmitt, 1979, pp. 54–5). This is clearly a different conception of 'social policy' from that found in the works of Titmuss (1958; 1968; 1974), T.H. Marshall (1975) and Boulding (1967). Even *within* countries there is considerable dissensus about the meaning of terms such as 'social policy', 'welfare' and 'social security'. As Kaim-Caudle observed, while 'social security' in America was normally used to describe Federal old-age, survivors, disability and health insurance programmes, an 'official' publication by the Department of Health, Education and Welfare used it to refer to all public programmes providing protection against loss of income as well as private occupational pension schemes and other private work-related benefits. In other 'official' Federal publications the term was not used at all (Kaim-Caudle, 1973, p. 6).

There are obviously serious definitional problems involved, therefore, in comparing social policies, either inter- or intra-nationally. Not all of these problems can be overcome, though they can be reduced by a careful definition of terms, and by identifying, as precisely as possible, exactly what is being compared with what. Nevertheless, the conclusions of any comparative study — especially if it is heavily reliant on quantitative data — should be regarded with some caution.

The second question, which Feldman raises, of what to compare and how to compare, is dealt with more fully in later sections of this book but we can readily see that the range of possibilities is very wide. Ironically, much of what we call comparative social policy consists of making contrasts and describing differences between countries and the ways in which they respond, and fail to respond, to social need. It is often more useful, and informative, to explore contrasts than to compare like with like. Studies of different systems of welfare widen our horizons, expose our cultural biases and set out a number of alternative policy responses. If our familiarity, for example, is only with the English educational system we may believe it to be the obvious and only type of structure for meeting educational needs. If, however, we look elsewhere to other countries with apparently similar needs but with different methods of meeting them we can begin to evaluate our own system more realistically, and in terms of a choice of policy alternatives.

Finally, there is the problem of competence. This is a crucial issue which is rarely discussed, perhaps out of professional pride or because it seems too obvious to mention. However, as Feldman points out:

> few scholars know enough about more than one country to venture into the detailed examination of public policy beyond one country's borders. (1978, pp. 293–4)

Consequently, existing comparative studies in social policy range from micro-analyses of programmes in one or two countries, or volumes with contributions from several authors on different countries (which do not actually *compare*) to research which involves rather superficial study of a large number of countries. A lack of competence in foreign languages is another obvious factor which will limit the extent of comparisons which can be drawn in social policy. Comparative research can founder, therefore, upon the most basic problems of expertise.

Many of these dilemmas are serious obstacles to comparative research but most of them are not necessarily insuperable. Nevertheless, they must lead us to conclude that comparative studies should be undertaken with due circumspection and that their results should be treated cautiously. The advantages of comparison in social policy can only be fully realized if the limitations of comparison are fully acknowledged.

Hugh Heclo wrote that when he began his research on income maintenance programmes in Britain and Sweden in 1967 'policy studies appeared a largely untended field of political science, and comparative studies seemed in a positively virginal state.' By 1972, however, when his research had been completed, the growth of interest in comparative research had been so rapid that he concluded 'the virgin is now threatened less with neglect and more with abuse' (1974, p. ix).

It is very important that, in attempting to advance comparative studies in social policy, we should not, inadvertently, abuse the virgin further.

Some approaches to comparison in social policy: a review of the literature

Even a brief review of the literature will reveal a very wide range of approaches to comparison in social policy. We can begin by identifying at least nine different orientations in comparative research. The categories enumerated below are not mutually exclusive and one study may simultaneously contain characteristics which can be identified with different categories. Nevertheless, it is possible (if only in a rather crude fashion) to identify different emphases in these studies which tend to locate them under one heading rather than another.

POLICY AREAS

This category covers many varied activities including studies in comparative education, comparisons of income maintenance programmes in different countries, for example, Heclo (1974) on Britain and Sweden, and Lawson and Young (1975) on Britain and West Germany; medical care in different societies (Anderson, 1972; Leichter, 1979) and housing and urban policy (Wendt, 1963; Fuerst, 1974; McKay, 1977). The collection of essays edited by Hayward and Watson (1975) offers a comprehensive review of planning in Britain, France and Italy, while Lawson and Reed (1975) look at both social security and medical care in the European Community. The emphasis is on cross-national comparison of broad policy areas.

PROBLEM AREAS

The studies here examine particular aspects of policy on an international basis. An obvious example is Titmuss' study of blood-giving practices in Britain, the United States, the USSR, South Africa and Japan (Titmuss, 1973). There is a growing literature on systems of payment for general practitioners and other health services (see Ashford, 1978, chapter 3). Glennerster's research on social service budgets in Britain and America (Glennerster, 1975) is another area of development, as is the work on housing subsidies in Britain and America (Mandelker, 1973) and on housing allowances in France and West Germany (Lawson and Stevens, 1974).

In addition to studies of specific policy areas there have also been attempts to use comparative research to investigate the definition and conceptualization of social problems such as poverty and crime (Townsend, 1970; Lawson and Young, 1975; Radzinowicz and King, 1977).

GROUPS IN NEED

In some cases, studies classified under this heading may overlap with the two categories above, although the orientation will often be rather different. Here we could point to the study of old people in three industrial societies by Shanas et al. (1967), and the work conducted by Cockburn and Heclo, for the Finer Committe, on services for one-parent families (Finer, 1974). Blackstone (1972; 1973) provides information on the care of pre-school children, while some of Sinfield's work on the unemployed (1968a; 1968b) has had a comparative emphasis.

THE SOCIAL POLICIES OF FOREIGN COUNTRIES

This category consists largely of descriptive studies of social welfare in countries which are not the author's own. Few of them are genuinely comparative or, alternatively, the points of contrast and comparison are implicit, and it is left to the reader to make links. Kaim-Caudle's study of *Social policy in the Irish Republic* (1967) and Bernice Madison's *Social welfare in the Soviet Union* (1968) are typical examples.

POLICY AREAS IN FOREIGN COUNTRIES

While the studies referred to above provide broad overviews of the social policies of foreign countries, the work under this heading has concentrated specifically on certain areas of policy. Again the research is, on the whole, not of a comparative nature and the implications (if any) for the writer's own country are not usually made explicit. Eckstein's study of the *English National Health Service* (1958) and Tony Lynes' work on *French pensions* (1967) are obvious examples, although there is some attempt, in the latter, to draw out lessons for Britain. Michael Ryan's study of *The organization of Soviet medical care* (1978) may also be included.

Under this heading there is another genre of work which does not claim to be comparative but which has been a significant contribution to the social policy literature. This is the research by foreign nationals on various aspects of British social policy. Apart from Eckstein's study of the health service there have been a series of penetrating accounts, including a study of the 1957 Rent Act (Barnett, 1969) and an analysis of social policy in the period 1914–39 (Gilbert, 1970; see also de Schweinitz, 1943; Gilbert, 1966). The work of such writers suggests that they bring three particular virtues to 'comparative' research. The insights of a foreigner, the insights of political scientists and, thirdly, they are often able to secure access to information which may have been denied to (or not so tenaciously pursued) indigenous writers.

COMPARISONS OF TOTAL WELFARE SPENDING

The research here has been almost entirely quantitative and, consequently, beset by many of the definitional problems outlined in the last section. Wilensky's more recent work (1975; 1976) fits into this category, as does some of the work of Kaim-Caudle (1973). Wilensky's work has been particularly wide-ranging based, as it is, on the analysis of 'crude, cross-sectional data on gross categories of welfare and military spending for sixty-four countries' (1975, p. xii). It is organized in terms of 'leaders, laggards and middle-rank spenders' in social welfare. OECD, the ILO, the US Department of Health, Education and Welfare and the United Nations have all produced research which compares total welfare spending, or particular aspects of welfare spending, in different countries. In recent years the data produced by the OECD and EEC has become increasingly sophisticated and these organizations have gone some way towards overcoming the methodological difficulties involved in collecting comparable statistical information.

COMPARISONS OVER TIME

There is a growing body of literature which compares developments in social policy over a period of time, both nationally and cross-nationally. Some of the work concentrates upon describing changes in policy and on identifying 'landmarks' of social legislation (Bruce,

1972; Fraser, 1973). The more interesting and useful historical accounts set policy developments into ideological and political contexts which highlight changing views about the role of the State, the role of State welfare and the interrelationships between public and private providers of welfare, amongst other issues (Saville, 1957; Goldthorpe, 1962; Briggs, 1961). Some of this work looks at historical developments in more than one country and attempts to relate them (Woodroofe, 1962; Mencher, 1967). Other research concentrates on changes in particular areas of policy, or the treatment of certain groups in need such as the unemployed (Harris, 1972), or at changing attitudes towards particular problems and policy responses to them (Deacon, 1976 on 'scrounging'; May, 1978 on 'family violence').

'DIFFERENT' AND 'SIMILAR' SYSTEMS

Some of the recent work in comparative policy studies, especially that of American political scientists, has adopted an approach which asks, essentially, how different/similar political systems respond to similar social problems and needs. The essays by Anderson, Teune and Marmor et al. in Ashford's book *Comparing public policies: new concepts and methods* (1978) illustrate this approach particularly well. Without necessarily using the terminology of political science previous works have looked, comparatively, at the societal, political and ideological determinants of problems and policies (Rimlinger, 1971; Wilensky and Lebeaux, 1965; Gough, 1975, Mishra, 1977; Navarro, 1977).

CONCEPTS AND ISSUES

This final category includes a wide variety of contributions which concentrate particularly on the examination of concepts and policy issues from a comparative perspective. Piven and Cloward (1972), for example, have examined the notion of social policy as a means of social control both historically and cross-nationally, as has Donajgrodzki (1977). I have also discussed this relationship in some of my own work (Higgins, 1978a; 1978b; 1980). Titmuss engaged in his study of blood-giving practices in five countries in order, partly, to examine the notion of altruism, while, in earlier works, he drew on comparative data to support his arguments about the drawbacks of private medical care (1968) and about the relative virtues of a legalistic and discretionary approach to welfare rights (1971). Most of the essays in Heidenheimer, Heclo and Adams (1976) look comparatively at important issues in social policy such as the role of interest groups in policy-making, and central-local relationships in the administration of welfare, while Bruno Stein has examined work and welfare in Britain and America (1976). This latter category, therefore, takes in a number of diverse debates.

This brief review of some of the main approaches to comparison in social policy is intended to show that there can be, and have been, many different answers to the question of 'how and what to compare'. Clearly, different circumstances require different approaches, and different questions need different methodological tools with which to answer them. There is no single 'comparative method', therefore, which is applicable to all contexts. Nevertheless, one can probably go further and argue that descriptive case studies which, in the past, have been the mainstay of comparative social policy have been much less informative than they might have been, because they have tended to lack a sense of perspective and context. In the end, many of them have told us little more than that different countries do things differently (or, occasionally, in the same way as we do). Little can be learned from such conclusions, on their own.

Another problem with descriptive studies is that there is sometimes a tendency, as Marmor and Bridges noted, to pick out, from comparative surveys, who 'does best' on particular issues. This they describe as the 'world series view of comparative research' (1977, p. 6). Such a perspective gives us few clues about why, or in what circumstances, some countries 'do better' than others in, for example, the care of the elderly or in their efforts to deal with the problem of poverty. On the whole, therefore, description is an important first step in comparative research but it should not (except in certain circumstances) be regarded as an end in itself. Similar remarks can be made about quantitative comparative data. It may be very useful, in some circumstances, to have information on — for example — per capita expenditure on health care. However, as Marmor and Bridges remark:

> since per capita expenditures determine neither the quality nor the mix of medical care services, it is not clear that anything crucial has been learned about medical care services when per capita expenditures are statistically explained. (1977, p. 10)

If we wish to understand the origins, style, delivery and distribution of medical care services in any country, therefore, we must look beyond per capita expenditures and other quantitative measures for our explanations.

Generally speaking, then, it is important to supplement descriptive case studies and quantitative data with more broadly based analyses which may help to 'explain' as well as describe. In the chapters which follow it will be clear that we tend to err on the side 'breadth' rather than 'depth', not because this is an inherently superior approach but because it offers the possibility of making better use of data already collected, as well as providing guidelines for any future comparative research.

CHAPTER 3

The Development of a Comparative Perspective

The importance of a comparative perspective can be seen when we attempt to explain the nature and functions of social policy in any society. Indeed, the *failure* to compare has, in the past, led to inaccurate accounts of how and why social programmes have developed in different societies. There has been a tendency to generalize from one or two particular cases and a tendency to conclude that the methods of meeting need with which we are familiar are the 'natural' and the 'normal' ones. In other disciplines in the social sciences the evidence of anthropologists and historians has shown, increasingly, that our preconceptions of how needs could, and should, be satisfied may not be valid for all societies. We now know, for example, that the nuclear family and serial monogamy are not the only ways of ordering personal relationships. Nor is there universal agreement on what constitutes a deviant or criminal act, and how it should be punished. It is important that similar comparative perspectives are introduced into the study of social policies so that we are in no danger of arguing, say, that the *obvious* way of dealing with dependent groups, such as the sick, the elderly and the unemployed, is through collective provision by the State. A variety of ways of meeting their needs can be identified in different historical periods, and in different societies, and it is important to consider these differences when looking for explanations of policy development.

How did this situation arise, and why is it that, in comparison with the other social sciences, the discipline of social policy and administration was so slow in developing theoretical insights and more broadly based explanations? Why was it that the so-called 'comparative method', already well-established in sociology and political science, was regarded either as an irrelevance or as the preserve of the occasional eccentric who derived a vicarious excitement from discovering what went on in foreign parts? Part of the explanation may lie in the fact that many of those, both inside and outside the discipline, saw it essentially as empirically orientated and concerned, primarily, with small-scale problem-solving. As Mishra remarked:

> the interest is not in knowledge of social welfare institutions, for its own sake, but rather in understanding the nature and dimensions of a particular social problem — for example poverty or homelessness — with a view to its solution. (1977, p. 3)

The tenor of the literature which the discipline was generating in the early post-war years, when the study of social policy was still in its infancy, was also an important factor. A brief examination of this literature helps to suggest why certain kinds of approach became dominant, why so little emphasis was placed on comparative research and how this led, in some cases, to inappropriate conclusions about the role of social policy in different contexts. In the pages which follow some of the main contributions to the literature are set out chronologically so that readers can see how the arguments actually developed, and how certain conclusions were reached. The purpose is not to catalogue a series of academic squabbles but to suggest why comparative research was neglected for so long and why we are still struggling in the foothills of comparative social policy rather than climbing the peaks.

'Social conscience' theories and the neglect of comparative research

For many of those writing during the 1950s, in Britain, their subject matter was essentially a description of the social services introduced in the late 1940s, and a series of legislative enactments designed to enhance social welfare. The main textbook on the subject was *The social services of modern England,* by Penelope Hall, which was first published in 1952. She had chapters on the health services and income maintenance programmes, on housing and town planning, and on social services for children and young people. She also included information on the care of the aged and handicapped and on ways of dealing with 'problem families'. The sections of the book which were confined to a simple description of the services available were largely unproblematic. However, those chapters which purported to 'explain' the development of these services were seriously misleading and set the pattern for an atheoretical approach to explanation in social policy which lacked any rigour and which persisted for many years.

Penelope Hall argued, for example, that:

> social service is essentially 'the manifestation of a personal interest in a human situation', a recognition of both the uniqueness and value of the individual, and of our common humanity. The basis of social service is then to be found in the obligation a person feels to help another in distress, which derives from the recognition that they are, in some sense, members one of another. (1957, pp. 3–4)

Unless Penelope Hall was suggesting, therefore, that these basic human values and sentiments were peculiarly English (and she did not appear to be doing so) it seemed reasonable to assume that, in most other countries too, they would be realized in the form of centrally organized services, provided for 'the common good'. In her view, the humanitarian impulse would — in time — lead to a recognition that all civilized societies had an obligation to provide for their dependent members. As for the particular configuration of services which, in Britain, came to be known as 'the Welfare State' she concluded:

> The Welfare State is a witness to the reality of our belief in community, as well as to our belief in the claims of the individual. The development of the social services and their integration in the Welfare State are then the outcome of the application of certain fundamental beliefs about the value of people as people and the significance of their relationships with each other. (Hall, 1957, p. 308)

From her initial concern with the social services of modern England Penelope Hall is drawn, in the closing paragraph of her book, to a series of conclusions about the need for Christian fellowship to inspire our attempts to integrate 'man and society'. Calling upon the teachings of St Paul and Albert Schweitzer she exhorts us to 'love one's neighbour as oneself' and to

> bring encouragement to those who, in different parts of the world, and in ways adjusted to their own culture, are seeking, often in circumstances of the greatest difficulty, to establish and

> maintain free co-operation based on respect for the individual as the basis of society. (1957, pp. 14–15)

Penelope Hall's book was typical of a genre of textbooks which advanced what John Baker has described as 'the social conscience thesis'. This approach maintained that:

> (1) Social policy manifests, through the state, the love that men have for each other. It is benevolent and is provided for the benefit of recipients and the community as a whole.
>
> (2) Changes in social policy result from two factors — a widening and deepening sense of social obligation, and an increase in our knowledge of need.
>
> (3) Changes are cumulative, and policy evolves constantly, though not evenly, in the direction of greater generosity and wider range.
>
> (4) Improvements are irreversible, and contemporary services are the highest historical form.
>
> (5) While present services are incomplete and defective, the central problems of social welfare have been solved, and society is now so constituted that we can look forward to further improvement. (Baker, 1979, p. 178)

The social conscience thesis has been, and in many cases still is, enormously influential amongst generations of students, not only social workers in training (for whom Hall's book was primarily written), but children pursuing 'humanities' and 'civics' courses in schools, as well as students of social administration in institutions of higher education, and practitioners in the social services. It is important, therefore, to consider the ways in which the analysis, put forward by Penelope Hall and others of like mind, has been misleading and to look for the implications for a comparative approach to the study of social policy.

Firstly, if reform and innovation in social policy are essentially a manifestation of basic human values, as social conscience writers contend, then one would expect that the expression of these values would take similar forms in all societies. Penelope Hall's particular brand of well-meaning ethnocentrism led her to argue (on the basis of little, or no, evidence):

> (a) That the "belief in the intrinsic value of human beings because

they are human, and belief in the reality of community" are, indeed, fundamental and universal human values.

(b) That they normally find their outlet in the provision of social services of various kinds.

(c) And that, by implication, social services are a universal phenomenon.

Secondly, in her over-emphasis on the impact of humanitarianism on the development of social services she considerably under-emphasizes (in fact, barely mentions) the importance of political constraints in the policy process. For example, in looking at the evolution of income maintenance and health care programmes she gives no weight to the significance of conflicting interests within the pre-war services. Little account is taken of the role of different pressure groups in the creation of the National Health Service, the enormous controversies which raged, and the factors which led to the compromise which emerged. Instead, she simply concludes:

> Thus, as with social insurance and assistance, so with provisions for medical care; the time was ripe for the creation of a unified national service based on the varied developments of the previous half-century. (1957, p. 61)

An account such as this which is so heavily dependent upon the assumption of 'good will' on the part of policy-makers and upon the belief that consensus rules supreme, inevitably overlooks certain important factors which must be considered when seeking *explanations* for decisions, policies and programmes. It typifies, *par excellence,* what Titmuss was to describe as 'the placid, conventional romance of the rise of the Welfare State' (quoted in Hay, 1975, p. 21).

At the same time, as long as present-day social programmes in Britain are measured in terms of their predecessors (rather than the programmes of other countries) the conclusion will invariably emerge that there has been a gradual improvement. As Baker observes:

> The criteria for the evaluation of the social services have tended not to be the concrete achievements of other societies but to be drawn from Britain. This too has added strength to the social conscience thesis. In looking backwards the analyst is bound to be struck by the progress made. (1979, p. 205)

Mishra raises a third problem which may result from the kind of approach to studying social policy which Penelope Hall represented. If, as we suggested, early work in the field of social administration was essentially pragmatic and concerned with solving specific social problems it was not surprising, he argues, that it should focus on national, or even local, conditions.

> Given this concern with amelioration — with the improvement of conditions — social administration is likely to concentrate on practical problems of social policy. Gauging the dimensions of a problem, evaluating past policy, making some implicit or explicit recommendation for future action have been and are likely to be the stock-in-trade of social administration. It follows that the centre of attention must be the national situation — for example, the problems and policies in Britain. (Mishra, 1977, p. 5)

Although this may partially explain the ethnocentrism of much writing on social administration, it is not necessarily the case that a discipline concerned primarily with problem-solving will only look inwards. There is a good deal of evidence to suggest that the need to solve a particular problem, at home, will often be a spur to comparative research. Lloyd-George and Churchill, for example, were both eager to discover how other countries, especially Germany, had solved the problems of devising a national insurance scheme. Indeed, Hay has argued that it was common practice, at the turn of the century, to examine the experience of other countries before deciding upon a particular course of action:

> After all, societies as diverse as Germany, the United States of America, Tsarist and later Soviet Russia, Australia and Uruguay were embarking on social legislation which contained many similar elements to the Liberal reforms, at roughly the same time. More over, foreign influences were extremely important in the origin of these reforms. Historians usually cite Lloyd George's famous journey to Germany in 1908, out of which came his ideas for national insurance. But surveys of foreign practices preceded most major legislation. (1975, p. 15)

Similarly, Rys has argued that the 'cultural diffusion factor' has been highly significant in the development of social policy:

> The most obvious carriers of this kind of diffusion are the social

> policy makers of different nations wrestling with the problem of extreme poverty in certain classes of their population. Thus, in the Middle Ages, we find European kings introducing public assistance measures applied abroad without necessarily obtaining the desired results. The Committee on Mendicity of the French Revolution studied extremely carefully the English Poor Law before submitting its proposals. Bismarck himself studied the example of France before deciding what kind of protection for old age his country should adopt. . . . This is a natural development, even more widespread at the present time, when it can be said that any major social security reform in any country is likely to involve a preliminary examination of foreign examples. (1964, p. 26)

More recently, the Finer Committee, established to consider the problems of one-parent families, commissioned comparative research in order to find out how other countries met the needs of this particular group. Towards the end of the 1960s the British government took a great interest in the programmes established in America as part of the War on Poverty — especially the experiments in compensatory education and community action. Similarly, American governmental and voluntary agencies have amassed extensive material on the ways in which other countries meet the health care needs of their citizens. As we have suggested (pp. 13–14), one of the main areas of development in comparative research has been in those parts of the literature concerned with lesson-learning and problem-solving.

Thus, although it can be seen that much early work in social administration centred upon pragmatic issues and was concerned primarily with the national situation, we should not conclude that the two are always inextricably interlinked. There is no inherent reason why a discipline concerned with finding solutions to social problems should not have a comparative element.

The 'end of ideology' and 'convergence' theses

Whether or not the ethnocentrism of British social policy was 'inevitable' we can see that it had two quite different outcomes, both of which were discussed by Dorothy Wedderburn in 'Facts and theories of the Welfare State'. This article, published in 1965, marks something of a turning point in attempts to analyse the functions of social policy in a comparative perspective. On the one hand, the failure to compare, systematically, the experiences of Britain with those of other countries had led many to conclude that that the 'welfare state' was 'an almost exclusively British phenomenon'. On the other hand (albeit some twenty years later), sociologists of various political persuasions concluded that:

> the welfare state is a common phenomenon of all capitalist societies. In its most extreme form this view maintains that the 'welfare state' is but one aspect of 'industrial society' as such, be it capitalist, communist or any other. It is part of the 'logic' of industrialisation which 'everywhere has its managers, its managed and a pattern of interaction'. (Wedderburn, 1965, p. 127)

The 'uniqueness' and 'universal phenomenon' perspectives sit uncomfortably beside each other in the literature. Asa Briggs, for example, in an article which attacked the 'placid, conventional romance' of earlier analyses of the development of the British Welfare State displays an ambivalence characteristic of many other writers. Although he criticizes the approaches in which 'the past was seen as leading inexorably along a broad highway with the "welfare state" as its destination' (1961, p. 222) he also claims *both* that the British experience was unique *and* that welfare states are features of all industrial societies. On the one hand, it is suggested that the 'Welfare State' legislation of 1945–50, in Britain, was the product of 'a particular set of circumstances' (p. 223) — especially the experience of war — while, in the next paragraph, it is argued that 'the uniqueness of Britain has been emphasized to the neglect of the study of trends and tendencies in other countries'. It is then suggested that the development of social programmes in Britain was both similar to and different from the development of such programmes elsewhere:

> In certain respects British experience has been unique, as foreign writers as different as Halevy and Schumpeter have recognized. The uniqueness can only be appreciated, however, when the experience of several countries is taken into account. The trends and tendencies which led journalists, politicians and historians to apply the label 'welfare state' to Britain may be noted in all modern, industrialised communities. (pp. 223–24)

Although the spirit of the rest of Briggs' article tends to support the view of the universality of welfare states, there is obvious confusion, in these passages, about the uniqueness or otherwise of the British Welfare State.

T.H. Marshall, attempting to grapple with the same question, is more confident of the uniqueness of the British experience:

> The British Welfare State of the 1940s was . . . the culmination of a long process which began in the last quarter of the nineteenth century, a process during which, as Mr Crossman puts it 'capitalism has been civilized'. But it was also the product of an explosion of forces which chance and history had brought together in Britain's unique experience in the war and in the transition to a state of peace. (1963, p. 287)

In short:

> The British Welfare State is unique because it was born in circumstances that were unique. (p. 279)

Despite his firm conviction, here, that the British experience was unique, Marshall argued — in another context — that industrialized societies showed a distinct pattern of convergence in their attitudes towards social policy. Marshall argues that experts, from Beveridge on, were concerned with 'applying techniques, which were of universal validity, to problems that were an intrinsic part of modern, industrial society' (1970, p. 61). The language which these experts used was an international language so that the result, in Marshall's view, was 'a marked convergence of social policy in all countries where social policy could be said to exist' (p. 62). Convergence could also be explained, he argued, as being 'the natural result of consolidation at the national level'. Using Britain and Germany as examples he shows how the former originally developed sickness and unemployment benefits, while the latter concentrated upon pensions and sickness benefit. Gradually, each borrowed ideas from the other so that 'it was natural that both countries, as they gained in experience, should fill in the gaps' (p. 62) and that 'after that the two systems merged very closely'.

Thus, although the naivety of earlier 'explanations' of the development of social policy had given way to more sophisticated analyses, which attempted to relate changes in social policy to other societal developments, a number of very real dilemmas were still apparent. By the beginning of the 1960s two trends had begun to emerge. Both can be attributed, in part, to the failure to adopt a systematic and rigorous approach to comparative research in social policy. Firstly, the failure to use comparative data at all had led some writers — largely on the basis of guesswork — to conclude that the British Welfare State was unique, while others were led to exactly the opposite conclusion, that welfare States were a universal phenomenon. Secondly, the use of some impressionistic and inadequately researched comparative data had led other writers to exactly the same conflicting conclusions so that a little, incomplete, learning also proved to be misleading.

Gradually, however, the view that welfare states were to be found in all industrialized, urbanized societies came to predominate (Kerr, 1962; Eyden, 1965; Zald, 1965). It was also linked, to some extent, with the 'end of ideology' debate which was the focus of one of the main controversies in sociology at that time. Where social policy was concerned it was argued that all advanced societies had, on the whole, accepted the principles of 'welfare statism'. Daniel Bell, whose book in 1960 was influential in the debate, argued, for example, that:

> there is, today, a rough consensus among intellectuals on political issues: the acceptance of a welfare state; the desirability of decentralized power; a system of mixed economy and of political pluralism. (1960, pp. 402–3)

Similarly, S.M. Lipset agreed that:

> the fundamental political problems of the industrial revolution have been solved: the workers have achieved industrial and political citizenship, the conservatives have accepted the welfare state and the democratic left has recognized that an increase in overall state power carries with it more dangers to freedom than solutions for economic problems. (1963, p. 406)

Overall, he concluded: 'the ideological issues dividing left and right (have) been reduced to a little more or less government ownership and economic planning' (p. 404).

It was suggested that the foundations of a welfare state had been laid, in most countries, in the late 1940s and early 1950s (if they had not been laid earlier). The debate, it was maintained, now centred not so much upon whether there should be welfare states, but upon what form they should take. Thus, T.H. Marshall is led to conclude:

'the issues at stake in the sixties turned out to be less concerned with social ideology than with social engineering' (1967, pp. 88–9). In a sense Marshall was both right and wrong in this conclusion (indeed he, himself, tacitly acknowledged this in rewriting the passage in subsequent editions of the book). He was right in arguing that there was a surprisingly broadly based consensus which accepted that welfare states were a universal phenomenon, and seemed an inevitable stage in the process of industrialization. Superficially the argument was persuasive. Advanced societies created new needs and new conditions of dependency (unemployment, increasing numbers of people living into old age; the demand for a healthy and literate workforce) which could no longer be dealt with adequately by the family or community. It seemed reasonable and logical, therefore, that the State should intervene to protect its citizens and to compensate them for unfavourable changes in their circumstances for which it was partly responsible. Thus, it was increasingly regarded as impracticable that issues such as the relief of poverty or the provision of medical care should be left to individual enterprise. It was a small step from here to the conclusion, expressed in a good deal of social policy literature, that the State *had* to act. This was an erroneous conclusion, again based on little or no historical or comparative evidence (which would have suggested otherwise). As we shall see, not only did the State *not have to* provide for the welfare of its citizens but in some periods, and in some countries, *it didn't*.

Whatever the validity of this perspective Marshall — at the time of writing — was probably right to suggest that most (though, of course, not all) writers seemed to be agreed that welfare states were both inevitable and universal features of advanced, industrialized societies. He was wrong, however, to argue that all the major ideological battles had been fought and won. Dissension now focused not so much on whether welfare states *did* exist but on whether they *should* exist in any permanent form.

Hostility to the notion of welfare states came from a group of writers often referred to (by, for example Wedderburn, 1965; George and Wilding, 1976) as 'anti-collectivists'. Essentially, they saw the welfare state as:

> a phase to be passed through at a particular stage of industrialization, but which can be increasingly dispensed with as output increases. (Wedderburn, 1965, p. 135)

One of them, Professor Peacock, insisted — in a much-quoted

phrase — that: 'the true object of the Welfare State is to teach people how to do without it' (quoted in Wedderburn, 1965, p. 136). Michael Fogarty argued that, inspired by Professor Peacock's words, 'Some economists have been contemplating a gradual winding-up of state services' (quoted in Seldon, 1961, p. 137). And that:

> economists and other social scientists in the 1960s will be increasingly concerned, not with the welfare state as we have come to think of it, but with the institutional structures that could be devised to take its place. (Quoted in Seldon, 1961, p. 137)

It is obvious, even from these brief remarks, that — in the early 1960s — the basic principles of the welfare state were still being challenged. There were also profound ideological differences between the supporters of 'welfare statism', and it was not the case that these could all be reduced to questions of 'social engineering'.

There had been, for some years, a growth in descriptive, comparative studies in social policy and in comparative research which sought to answer specific policy problems. However, it was the claim that welfare states were 'inevitable' (and, as some argued, 'functionally necessary') in industrial society which gave the real impetus to comparative research in social policy — or, at least, to the type of comparative research which was concerned with 'explanation' rather than description. Several writers began to question the rather glib assertions about the universal incidence of welfare states and began to apply the tools of sociological and political theory to issues which had, hitherto, been accepted uncritically. The critique was helped by its association with some of the debates in mainstream sociology. Writers such as Goldthorpe (1962; 1964), Titmuss (1965), Wedderburn (1965), and later Carrier and Kendall (1973), Mishra (1973; 1975; 1976; 1977) and George and Wilding (1976) all observed that the 'inevitability' argument in social policy was beset by many of the problems of functionalist analysis and that it implied a 'convergence' in industrial societies which needed further examination. Furthermore, the argument could *only* be proven or disproven if comparisons were made between industrial and non-industrial societies, between different industrial societies or between industrial societies at different stages of development.

Goldthorpe, in articles published in 1962 and 1964, was one of the first writers to examine, systematically, the assertion that ideological differences had been resolved and that the 'logic of industrialism' had led to a pattern of convergence between industrial societies in which the value of State-provided welfare programmes was widely accepted. In the first of these articles he questioned the line of argument which held that, 'a particular social problem "*had* to be dealt with" or that a particular piece of legislation was "imperative" or "inevitable" ', and hence the view that, 'in an industrial society . . . some form of social policy is "necessary" ' (1962, p. 53). In the later article he drew on evidence from Britain, America and Russia to show that all industrial societies have not developed along the same lines and that convergence theories had been too deterministic. Quoting Myrdal, for example, he suggested that America — unlike most European countries — had failed to establish comprehensive welfare programmes:

> In particular he [Myrdal] stresses the inadequate achievement of government in America in long-range economic planning, in redistributional reforms, and in the provision of public services and advanced social welfare schemes. (1964, p. 105)

Secondly, Goldthorpe was critical of convergence theorists for their overemphasis on the 'logic of industrialism' and their failure to take account of conflicting values and ideologies in determining the direction in which different industrial societies have developed. His third criticism was that convergence theorists have relied too heavily upon their own experience, and had failed to gather sufficient comparative data to test out their assertions. Goldthorpe concluded that:

> finally, and perhaps most culpably, there is the ethnocentric bias; that failure of the imagination which leads the sociologist to accept his own form of society, or rather some idealised version of this as the goal towards which all humanity is moving. (1964, p. 117)

In the following year, 1965, Dorothy Wedderburn also attacked the view that welfare states were simply part of the 'logic of industrialism', and were common to all industrial societies. In particular, she argued, America did not appear to display the same commitment, evident in most European countries, to ensuring minimum social welfare provisions. 'Insufficient attention has been given', she wrote, 'to the extent to which America is outside the mainstream of capitalist societies in so far as welfare state provisions are concerned' (pp. 129–30). Listing the inadequacies, or, in some cases, the lack of, Federal schemes for the elderly, the sick, low wage earners and the unemployed, she concludes, 'in the light of these deficiencies it is questionable how far the phenomenon of the welfare state can be said to exist in the U.S.A.' (p. 130). Carrier and Kendall (1973, p. 214) presented further evidence on countries including South Africa and New Zealand, which also undermined the oversimplified thesis that welfare states necessarily develop as a by-product of industrialization.

The 'end of ideology' and 'convergence' theses were, thus, shown to have distinct limitations as 'explanations' of the role of social policy (or 'welfare states') in industrial society. Richard Titmuss (1965) showed that the complacency which they engendered also had serious practical implications for policy. The 'end of ideology writers', he claimed, 'imply, directly or indirectly, that inequality is no longer an issue for our societies' (1965, p. 318). This meant that, in policy terms:

> Incrementalism in social welfare is approved: small-scale programmes for small-scale problems. These observers of the scene do not raise questions about values and goals, indeed, they deny the need for basic changes. So the concern is to find better means whereby administrators, psychologists and social workers can help and counsel the minority poor to abandon the 'culture of poverty'.

On Lipset's view (quoted earlier) that the problems of the industrial revolution had been solved, and that parties of all political complexions accepted the welfare state, Titmuss concluded:

> It is conceivable that this statement may serve historians as a summing up of majority opinion in the 1950s, but from the perspective of 1965 it is, to say the least, a dubious proposition. (1965, p. 319)

Thus, we can see that the 'social conscience' theories of the late 1950s, which argued that humanitarianism was the main spur to the development of social policy, were overtaken in the early 1960s by 'convergence' and 'end of ideology' theories which claimed that welfare states developed 'necessarily' and 'inevitably' as part of the 'logic of industrialism'. It was claimed that industrial societies displayed increasingly similar institutional arrangements, that they were also converging in their attitudes towards social problems and that all had reached more or less the same conclusions about how to deal with them. Both types of approach were misleading, and both were weakened by their tendency to generalize from particular situations and their conclusion that what they observed in one context was true for all industrialized societies. It was rapidly becoming clear, even from a superficial examination of different societies, that a wide range of policy responses to social need had evolved since the nineteenth century. Comparisons between different European countries, between Europe and America, and with such countries as Russia and Japan, indicated that the convergence thesis had grossly oversimplified the patterns of development in social policy and could not account for the diverse approaches which were increasingly in evidence.

Although analysts such as Rimlinger (1971), Wilensky (1975; 1976) and Mishra (1976; 1977) still differed in their conclusions about the extent to which the convergence thesis could be sustained (and under what conditions) it was at least understood, by this stage, that the only way to examine the role of social policy in industrial societies was by comparative research. Some of these disagreements sprang from differences in definitions (of 'social policy', 'state welfare', 'welfare state', etc.), while others were due to differences of opinion over what developments should be taken as evidence of convergence. For example, if we looked at the scale of the increase in public expenditure on social welfare in America since the mid-1960s we might conclude that the United States was moving, at great speed, towards becoming a 'welfare state' on the European model. If, however, we examined delivery systems in social programmes, voting behaviour and attitudes to welfare we would probably conclude that, in this same period, America had moved significantly towards the political Right and that the principles of 'welfare statism' were widely regarded as abhorrent. In other words, although there has been an expansion of publicly financed welfare this has not been accompanied by a growth in attitudes which favour the establishment of a welfare State.

Overall, however, the evidence which was being collected from a variety of different industrialized countries demonstrated that there were still fundamental differences in practice with respect to social policy. Thus Mishra concludes:

> There are no good grounds to suppose that advanced industrial

> society spells the end of ideology — that culture, political beliefs, class interests, historical continuities and the like cease to influence social structure. Nor does evidence bear out the thesis of increasing similarity of social policy to any great extent. Looking at the patterns of welfare in advanced industrial countries what we find is a measure of similarity and difference and little evidence of the latter disappearing. True, a 'weak' thesis of convergence can be sustained; thus in all Western industrial countries the state has assumed greater responsibility for meeting needs and occupational welfare has also become more prominent. But this still leaves scope for a great deal of diversity in welfare patterns, for example in respect of the mix between these two types of provision. (1977, p. 40)

This present book is based on the belief that both similarities and differences do, indeed, exist in the social policies of industrialized countries, and that it is important, both in terms of 'understanding' and 'explanation' to study them. The debate about whether other countries have a 'welfare state' such as we know it in Britain — quite apart from the question of whether Britain is the appropriate 'benchmark' — now seems redundant. It is fairly clear that most countries, on which we have data, do have social policies — even if, in some cases, the policy is *not* to act, or not to encourage State intervention in social welfare. The problem for the student, if he/she cannot assume that the social welfare system of his/her own country is replicated elsewhere, is how to make sense of these different practices and how to determine which factors he/she should concentrate upon. The rest of this book is designed to provide a few clues and some answers to these questions.

Models of welfare

The first problem to which some attention has been given in the literature is that of the selection of broad categories which might be used to identify, and to some extent classify, the differences of approach to policy and the varieties of response to social need. Perhaps the most widely used categorization is that developed by Wilensky and Lebeaux in 1965. They devised two 'models of welfare', the *residual* and the *institutional*, as a means of conceptualizing the two dominant approaches to social work in the United States. However, their original formulation has since been used by other writers, on a wider basis, to represent the two ends of a continuum of social welfare activities in different societies (Pinker, 1971; Titmuss, 1974; Butterworth and Holman, 1975; Mishra, 1977). Wilensky and Lebeaux defined the boundaries of the two models as follows:

> The first (residual) holds that social welfare institutions should come into play only when the normal structures of supply, the family and the market break down. The second (institutional), in contrast, sees the welfare services as normal 'first line' functions of modern industrial society. . . . They represent a compromise between the values of economic individualism and free enterprise, on the one hand, and security, equality and humanitarianism on the other. (1965, pp. 138–9)

Before we can use such models, however, we must decide what questions we need to ask in order to allocate sets of social policies to their appropriate category. Titmuss (1968, p. 30) suggests that we begin by looking at three central issues:

> (a) What is the nature of entitlement to use? Is it legal, contractual or contributory, financial, discretionary or professionally determined entitlement?
>
> (b) Who is entitled and on what conditions? Is account taken of individual characteristics or social-biological characteristics? What, in fact, are the rules of entitlement? Are they specific and contractual — like a right based on age — or are they variable, arbitrary or discretionary?
>
> (c) What methods, financial and administrative, are employed in the determination of access, utilization, allocation and payment?

Next, Titmuss argues, we should look at the functions which social policies aim to fulfill. Some are designed as compensation for socially caused 'diswelfares', while others (such as education) are seen as an investment for the future. Some intend to maximize personal 'command-over-resources' while others are expected, primarily, to fulfill integrative functions, to create harmony and discourage conflict (1968, pp. 130–1). The answers to such questions, he concludes, represent:

> little more than an elementary and partial structure map which

> can assist in the understanding of the welfare complex today. . . . A more sophisticated (inch to the mile) guide is essential for anything approaching a thorough analysis of the actual functioning of welfare benefit systems. (p. 131)

Although there are certain limitations to employing institutional and residual models of welfare, they can act as a useful starting point for comparative research. Generally speaking, we can see that the social policies of different countries conform, more or less, to one pattern rather than the other. We can also, as Mishra does (1977, p. 91) fill out the models by including other criteria by which to judge social policies. In the residual model, for example, State intervention is minimal rather than optimal. Similarly, in fixing benefit levels, the State will aim to provide only the bare essentials to maintain subsistence (if that) rather than viewing welfare as conferring maximum opportunities, of achieving social equality and of guaranteeing freedom from want. The residual model is characterized by its emphasis on deterrence, by the stigmatizing qualities of those meagre benefits which do exist, and by the widespread use of means tests designed to reduce demand and to sift out the 'undeserving poor'. In the residual model the range and coverage of services is low and there are large areas of unmet need. Voluntary organizations, privately funded institutions and the family will be seen as the appropriate sources of assistance for most contingencies, and the State is regarded as the 'provider of last resort'. There will be a tendency to offer benefits in kind rather than in cash so that recipients are less able to 'misuse' their benefits, or to use them for purposes which were not intended. The principles of the institutional model are the converse of those above. Benefits are provided at an optimum level and are viewed as one of the 'rights of citizenship'.

Obviously these models are caricatures, to some extent, and it is impossible to find a country where social policies conform to one or the other in every respect. For example, we might argue that — at the time of writing — the United States conforms broadly to the residual model of welfare and Britain to the institutional model. The American system works largely on the assumption that State intervention — whether at the Federal, State or local level — should be at a minimum. The level of benefits in many Federal welfare programmes is extremely low, and often below the 'official' poverty line set by the Federal Government. There is no right to medical care for many groups of the population and the majority resort to private insurance schemes in order to pay for the health services they require. The standards in public housing are so bad as to act as a considerable deterrent to all but the most desperate applicants and consequently there is stigma attached to those who do find themselves housed by public authorities. On these criteria, therefore, one might conclude that America fits unequivocally into the residual model. However, we must add a number of qualifications. First of all, there really is no 'American system' of social policy, as such. Much of the responsibility for social programme is devolved to the State or local level, so that there are wide regional variations in the services offered. Some States, traditionally those in the north east and California, have more liberal attitudes to social welfare than others and choose to pay benefits at more generous levels than the Federal minimum. Secondly, the range of services offered by the various agencies of government is much broader than in many of those countries of Western Europe which are normally regarded as pursuing an institutional model of welfare. Certainly their coverage is limited and they may also be funded on an experimental or short-term basis but, in terms of numbers, they form an impressive array. Although we might conclude, therefore, that social policy in America is located nearer the end of the continuum represented by the residual model of welfare, we can see that it possesses some characteristics usually associated with the institutional model.

Using the same criteria we might regard Britain as conforming, fairly closely, to the institutional model of welfare but again there are reservations. Although many basic services, such as education and medical care, have been provided more or less free of charge since the 1940s, fees for drugs and medical prescriptions have gradually been reintroduced. There have also been moves, in recent years, to extend the private market in education, health, income maintenance and housing, at the same time as reducing expenditure on public services. Equally, certain areas of policy — for example, the treatment of the unemployed — clearly aim for minimum rather then optimum standards. On this basis, therefore, many would argue that what we see in Britain in the 1980s is a 'withering away of the Welfare State' and a movement away from the institutional model of welfare.

These two illustrations show, therefore, that although Wilensky's and Lebeaux's conceptualization of contrasting approaches to welfare is very useful in conveying a general 'feel' about the social policies of different countries, these are not precise measures. Apart from the other reservations we have expressed there is also the problem that the general orientation of a country's social policies can change quite dramatically within a very short space of time. The different approaches to social policy of Presidents Kennedy, Johnson and Nixon — in less than ten years — amply illustrates this point as do the shifting emphases of Labour and Conservative governments in Britain in recent years.

The philosophy which inspires a country's social policies is constantly being modified, sometimes only marginally, but at other times quite significantly. This means that the social policies of different societies correspond more closely to the models in some periods than in others. Pinker has also shown that the effects of 'institutionalist' and 'residualist' policies may not always differ very greatly in practice. Economic and political constraints and the need to compromise can sometimes mean that there is periodic convergence between the two extremes:

> So long as conditions of scarcity prevail and demand potentially exceeds the supply of social services, forms of rationing prevail. The institutionist begins with a generosity and is driven reluctantly towards stringency in allocation. The residualist starts with stringency and is driven reluctantly towards generosity. (1971, p. 107)

There is also the danger that models of this type will oversimplify — to the extent of serious misrepresentation — the various trends, conflicts and cross-currents which a more detailed examination of social policies would reveal. As Titmuss observed:

> The more one attempts to study the international literature about different national social policy institutions, the more one becomes aware of the diversity and complexity. The more one understands this complexity, the more difficult does it become to generalise (to simplify pragmatically) about the different roles that social services are supposed to play — and do actually play — in different countries. (1974, pp. 16–17)

However, as Titmuss goes on to say later in the book, the great value of using social policy models is that they can help to point us towards important lines of enquiry. 'With all their apparent remoteness from reality', he explains, they can 'serve a purpose in providing us with an ideological framework which may stimulate us to ask the significant questions and expose the significant choices' (1974, p. 136).

Going back to the analogy we used earlier we can see that the approach of the detective and that of the sociologist are again similar. The detective will find it useful to have such details of the criminal as his height, weight, colour of hair and manner of dress. However, this information — in itself — does not tell him who the villain actually is; at best it may give him some indication of what *kind* of man he is. To find out his identity he will need more detailed information from eyewitnesses, blood tests, fingerprints or photographs. Similarly, the sociologist is interested in such dimensions as the scope and philosophy of social policy in the countries he studies, but this sort of information can only provide him with a number of 'leads' which have to be followed up in much greater detail for the picture to be complete.

Assuming that the sociologist does not want to know all about every aspect of all social policies (even if he/she were capable of finding out) the next problem he/she faces is to decide what kind of information he/she does need, which of the facts are relevant to the case and what particular questions he/she is trying to answer. As we suggested in chapter 1, one useful starting point might be to ask such broad questions as 'what ideological influences — political, religious, etc. — determine the "shape" of social policy?', 'how do the world of work and the world of welfare interrelate?' and 'what "mix" of public and private systems of welfare is regarded as appropriate?' It is to some of these issues we now turn.

CHAPTER 4

Determinants of Social Policy I: The Role of the State

One of the curious and fascinating questions which arises when we begin to compare social policies in different countries, or in different historical periods, is why there should be such an enormous variety of responses to what, on the face of it, appear to be similar states of need. Most countries, for example, are faced with the problems of how to educate their workforce and of how to deal with those who cease to be part of the workforce by reason of ill-health, old age or shortage of employment opportunities. Similarly, all governments must consider the question of how to feed, house and ensure the physical and mental well-being of their people; yet no two countries have chosen the same solutions to these problems, and even within individual countries ideas about alternative solutions are constantly changing.

We have to ask, therefore, what determines the attitudes of governments, and other social welfare institutions, to the satisfaction of need. What makes them settle on a particular formula for meeting, or in some cases *not* meeting, needs, and how do they fix their priorities about the urgency of different needs? We also need to know why, in some countries, functions which are performed by statutory bodies and governmental agencies are seen, in others, as being the preserve of voluntary agencies. In short, if we were to take a snapshot of the social welfare system of any country, at any point in time, we need to know how certain features of the picture come to be as they are. Obviously, we cannot give our attention to all the details but it is possible to pick out a number of items which seem to be of special importance.

There are several questions we can ask in our pursuit of information about how particular attitudes to social policy are formed and how different ideologies of welfare come to be shaped and fashioned. Two important factors relate to the political and economic organization of societies. One of the key variables in determining who pays for welfare programmes, and how, and who provides such programmes is the actual organization of central and local government. It is important to know whether governmental responsibilities (including taxation and other forms of 'fund raising') are devolved to small local bodies or whether powers and responsibilities are largely concentrated in a central authority. It is also important to discover whether the State is generally regarded as being the provider of last, or first, resort. Would individuals normally look to the State as the obvious source of support in whom all powers have been vested or would they only seek State assistance when all the other alternatives (of self-help, private endeavour, charity, etc.) had failed?

Another variable is the socio-economic organization of the society we are studying. Is it predominantly rural or urban? Is it totalitarian, communist, liberal-democratic, social-democratic, conservative? What particular form of economic system is dominant? It is primarily a collectivist economy or do capitalism, *laissez-faire* and the private market flourish? A further question which has received relatively little attention in the literature on comparative social policy (and which is therefore explored at some length in a later chapter) is about the influence of religion upon social policy. The overriding importance of the Church's attitude to welfare issues can most clearly be seen in Catholic countries such as Italy and Eire, although other religious influences have obviously played their part in other societies. We are interested not only in the ways in which religious doctrine dictates guidelines for social policy, but also in the extent to which the Church itself acts as a provider of welfare. These are just some of the issues raised in this chapter (and later chapters) in attemping to identify the main determinants of social policy and to explain how different ideologies have arisen and the effects they have had on social policy.

The search for answers: the broader view

Various attempts have been made to elucidate broad patterns of development in social policy in industrialized societies (see Rys, 1964; Cutwright, 1965; Kaim-Caudle, 1973; Heclo, 1974; Heidenheimer et al., 1976). They sprang partly from a desire to either support or disprove convergence theories of social development. Of necessity they offer breadth rather than depth and obviously, in that respect, have certain limitations. One such attempt to identify the main determinants of the differences and similarities in the 'national welfare effort' has been made by Wilensky (1975). His hypothesis is that:

> differences between the welfare state leaders and laggards can be explained by specific differences in political, social and economic organization — by the degree of centralization of government, the shape of the stratification order and related mobility rates, the organization of the working class and the position of the military. (p. XIV)

It is also necessary to take into account, he argues, both, 'the length of time a country has been in the welfare business and the age composition of its population' (p. 9).

Perhaps the most important (negative) conclusion of Wilensky's research is his view that ideological factors are largely irrelevant as determinants of social policy. He claims that the type and broad character of both the political system and the economic system are of little or no importance in shaping the nature and outcomes of social policy. He argues, for example, that:

> the two dominant modern systems, totalitarianism and liberal democracy, work in the same direction — boosting spending a bit — via their influence on demographic structure.
>
> . . . on the basis of Pryor's comparison of seven market economies and seven centralized economies (1968), we can conclude that economic system too is irrelevant. (1975, pp. 48–9)

Although 'all rich countries develop a similar set of conflicting values and beliefs' about social welfare, the net effect, he suggests is that these 'welfare state ideologies' cancel each other out and have no overall influence.

Having identified what he refers to as the 'severe limits of global concepts of ideology' (p. 51) Wilensky then goes on to develop a number of 'structural explanations in the middle range' which aim to identify the specific attributes of social, political and economic organization which *do* affect the development of social policy.

In particular he argues that the more centralized the political system, the higher will be public spending on social welfare and the greater the emphasis on 'equality'. Secondly, the greater the degree of homogeneity within the population the more progress will be made in the development of welfare programmes. Anti-welfare attitudes, on the other hand, are likely to be evident where there is a high level of affluence, and of educational opportunity and occupational mobility. Similarly, the more numerous are the self-employed and the greater the availability of private welfare benefits the more hostility there will be to public welfare. Finally, the existence of large, strongly organized working-class movements with high degrees of participation will foster pro-welfare ideologies and high levels of public expenditure on social welfare (Wilensky, 1975, pp. 52–69).

His main emphasis is on the level of economic development as the key determinant of social policy.

> Over the long pull economic level is the root cause of welfare state development, but its effects are felt chiefly through demographic changes of the past century and the momentum of the programmes themselves once established. (p. 47)

Wilensky's approach essentially takes a consensual view which underplays the importance of conflict, and conflicting ideologies, in the development of State welfare. Much of the evidence he presents is intended to support the view that all industrializing countries display convergent patterns of social planning and social provision so that 'social security growth' is seen as 'a natural accompaniment of economic growth and its demographic outcome' (p. 47). However, as we argued in the last chapter and will illustrate further in the next section, there is contrary evidence to suggest that public social welfare provisions are not a universal and inevitable concomitant of economic growth.

Castles and McKinlay (1979) have attacked the kind of conclusions reached by Wilensky and others on a number of grounds. They are concerned, primarily, to refute the contention that 'politics does not matter'. This proposition, they argue, directly contradicts the conclusions of a number of writers who have shown that the character of the political system clearly determines the extent and nature of social welfare provision in certain cases. Using the example of Scandinavia they claim that:

> a substantial number of Scandinavian commentators have more

or less explicitly attributed high levels of welfare to the dominant role of the social democratic parties in Denmark, Norway and Sweden over the last half century. (p. 160)

As well as trying to demonstrate that the dominance of social democratic parties favours the development of public welfare, however, Castles and McKinlay also explore the hypothesis that: 'the level of public welfare decreases with the size of the vote for the major party of the Right' (p. 166). On the basis of evidence from 19 countries they conclude quite firmly that 'a small party of the Right is a necessary condition of high levels of welfare provision' (p. 168) and that 'politics does matter'. The absence of a major party of the Right does not, however, guarantee the development of social welfare. In countries which have a higher level of provision than one might expect, given the size of the right-wing vote, the influence of other factors must obviously be considered. In the case of Scandinavia, Castles and McKinlay argue that it is the strength and unity of working-class movements which has augmented the demand for public welfare. In countries which have a lower level of welfare than might be expected from the size of the right-wing vote (Belgium, Luxembourg, Switzerland and Finland) the explanation is said to lie in the existence of internal religious and linguistic fragmentation (p. 169).

Some of the criticisms which Castles and McKinlay level at Wilensky can also be made of Kaim-Caudle (1973) in his ten-country study of social security systems. The neglect of political determinants of social policy is partly explicable in this case because he deliberately chose ten countries which shared 'common political characteristics' (p. 14). These included the fact that all were democracies with governments placed in office by elections which were held every 3, 4 and 5 years. There was adult suffrage, secret ballots, freedom of the press and opposition to government. All had fairly stable governments and six of the ten were English-speaking. Overall, the ten countries (Austria, West Germany, Ireland, United Kingdom, Denmark, the Netherlands, Canada, United States, New Zealand and Australia) are described as being 'reasonably homogeneous' (p. 16). Controlling for the political dimension, then, Kaim-Caudle concludes that the three main determinants of social policy are

(i) demographic factors (such as population growth, birth, mortality and fertility rates),

(ii) economic factors (the rate of growth per capita and regional dispersal of income), and
(iii) policy considerations (whether to develop 'universal' or 'selective' benefits, whether to tolerate a private market in social security, whether benefits should be earnings-related, etc.).

Although he accepts the influence of some pressure groups on policy and the influence of opposition parties on public opinion his view of political influences generally is that, 'party-political ideology in the democratic countries with which this study is concerned is not as important as shaping social legislation as may appear' (p. 45). However, little evidence is brought forward to support this assertion and we might reasonably question the actual homogeneity of the countries to which Kaim-Caudle refers. We can show, for instance, that there is not only considerable heterogeneity *within* some of these countries (as Castles and McKinlay suggest) but that there are also certain important differences between them. Furthermore these distinctions are reflected in social policy. So, for example, successive political parties in government in the United Kingdom and United States since the 1950s have been responsible for substantial shifts in emphasis (from punitive and deterrent programmes to liberal and generous policies and back once more to selectivist, regressive programmes). There will be disagreements between different observers about whether these shifts in emphasis were sufficiently profound to alter, fundamentally, the social welfare systems in these two countries or whether they were merely 'fringe' concerns. Nevertheless, we can see that, both in principle and in practice, the development of social policy in these years was significantly influenced by different party-political ideologies.

A more comprehensive and more satisfactory analysis of the influences upon social policy is that offered by Vladimir Rys (1964). He identifies a wide range of variables which he allocates to two groups 'the predominantly internal factors' and 'the predominantly external factors'. At the same time he recognizes that these are not discrete categories and there may be several overlaps. The *predominantly internal factors* include:

(a) the demographic factor (b) the economic factor (c) the social structure factor (d) the political factor (e) the pressure group factor (f) the institutional evolution factor and (g) the social psychology factor. (p. 4) while the *predominantly external factors* include:

> (a) the cultural diffusion factor (b) the technical development factor (c) the international standardization and technical assistance factor and (d) the international co-operation factor. (p. 4)

We have already referred to most of the influences described as 'predominantly internal factors' and it is his exploration of the 'predominantly external factors' which particularly distinguishes the contribution of Rys from other writers in this field. His discussion of the 'cultural diffusion factor' is especially interesting. Ideas and techniques of social insurance are transmitted cross-culturally, he argues, at different levels and by different institutions. Policy-makers in one country may study the systems of other countries in order to learn lessons from them. There may be an exchange of ideas about social policy between political parties of several nations. There is also the rather special case of colonization. As Rys remarks:

> the process of social security diffusion through colonization inevitably starts by the colonial power granting various social amenities to its own citizens; in due time these advantages are extended to cover the native population either before or after the independence of these nations. (1964, p. 27)

A more contemporary example of the importance of 'cultural diffusion' in the design of social programmes is the policy of 'harmonization' adopted by the countries of the EEC.

In his discussion of 'external factors' Rys also refers to the facilitating role of international organizations in informing one country of developments in another, and in the provision of technical expertise and assistance.

From this array of factors Rys, like Castles and McKinlay and a number of other policy analysts and political scientists, identifies the political factor as being the single most significant determinant of social security systems and social policy generally:

> we have to conclude that the political factor represents the most important 'environmental' element in the evolution of social security: the demographic, economic, social structure or psychology factors, all have to be transposed to the political level at which legislative decisions are taken. Under these circumstances it may not be unjustified to conceive of the political factor as the

> sum total of all other social factors involved, and to consider social security as a political problem before anything else. (p. 19)

It is clearly in the political realm, and in the institutions of government, that the influences of the many other possible determinants of social policy become translated into policy proposals and ultimately into practice. The political dimension cannot, therefore, be ignored and should not be underestimated when looking at the social policies of different countries.

Heidenheimer, Heclo and Adams (1976) have also addressed themselves to the question of why countries should have differed so greatly in the priority which they give to certain types of public provision and the factors which affect their choice. They, too, point to the importance of class and ideology as being significant influences:

> Differences in class structure and ideology have been important factors. Some countries have had a 'protectionist' and collectivist ideology, while others were inclined to laissez-faire and individualism. If protectionist and collectivist values were strong, as in late nineteenth-century Germany, both employer and union organizations, conservative as well as socialist parties, tended to be more in favour of public provision of welfare goods. Similarly, where class structure was relatively rigid, pressures were strongest for the adoption of large-scale social services. In Britain and Sweden collective demands were advanced through trade unions and socialist political parties on bchalf of families, worker groups and classes. Moreover, some of these organizations themselves established important prototypes of social services. In Britain national health insurance was built on the self-help programs of the 'Friendly Societies', and in Sweden national housing policy was built on precedents set by union-sponsored housing co-operatives. (pp. 7–8)

Heidenheimer, Helco and Adams echo a number of other writers in emphasizing the importance of class, ideology and, to some extent, party. They explore the interaction of these different factors with respect to particular policy areas, using illustrations primarily from Britain, Sweden, West Germany and the United States.

This brief review of some of the research which has examined the various influences on social policy obviously opens up a wide range of possible issues which could be discussed in chapters on the determinants of social policy. Two factors have been singled out as being of particular interest, although not because they are necessarily the most important determinants in every case. Firstly, we discuss the 'role of the State', partly as a background to the later chapter on public and private systems of welfare and partly because it is a key variable in every social welfare system, and in discussing it a number of important related issues are raised. We focus particularly on the case of the United States as being a country in which the role traditionally assigned to the State has been relatively minimal. Secondly, we examine the influence of religion upon social policy, both at the theoretical and at the pragmatic level. The religious factor has been selected for further examination, apart from the intellectual challenge which it poses, primarily because there is rather little consideration, in the social policy literature, of its potential importance.

Those parts of the sociological literature, from Weber and Tawney on, which *have* examined religion in its social context have shown it to be of great significance in the development of capitalist societies. At the very least, therefore, it must be considered as one of a range of possible factors which have played a part in the development of systems of social welfare.

It will be clear from the above discussion that we are not in a position to declare conclusively which particular determinants of social policy are the most important and the most universal. It is also clear that we cannot generalize about the dominant influences which shape social policy. Although general observations may help to create an overall framework for the discussion, they must be tested against the evidence in each particular country or policy area which we are studying. The student should begin from the assumption that all factors are potentially relevant and should eliminate some of them and accord others particular significance only on the basis of empirical observation. He/she will rarely be in a position to explore most (or even any) of the factors, we have listed above, in depth. The main point is that he/she should be aware of the range of possible influences which may be important. In other words, he/she should line up all the suspects before deciding which one is guilty.

The role of the State: the case of America

One of the most important differences between countries lies in the role accorded to the State as a provider of welfare. Generally speaking, in the last 100 years, the position of governmental authorities both in making social policy and in the actual provision of services has increased in importance in most countries. However, this has not been a uniform development, and the reasons why State involvement has, or in some cases has not, grown during this period have not always been the same. In some countries, such as America, there is still a heavy reliance on voluntary agencies and self-help. Why should this be the case? Why should America be regarded by most writers as a 'reluctant welfare state'?

Japan may also be seen as an exception to the general picture of extensive State involvement in social welfare, as may Eire, although the explanations of why this should be are different in each case and are rooted in differences in culture, political beliefs, industrial organization and religious dogma. The sociologist as detective, therefore, will be asking both a 'what' and a 'why' question. What is the role of the State in the social welfare system and why does it occupy this particular role?

It may be useful to begin by looking at the case of America because although in recent years anti-welfare attitudes have been more in evidence and appear more intransigent than in most comparable countries it is by no means obvious that this was inevitable. The origins of American attitudes to social welfare (as elsewhere) have a peculiar, complex and intriguing history. While certain factors favoured an anti-welfare ethos from a very early stage in the development of modern American society others indicated that America might well adopt the European model of welfare provision.

One of the strongest influences working against the establishment of a powerful central government and a co-ordinated national policy on social welfare lay in the very origins of the American nation itself. Incorporation of the thirteen colonies, Gronbjerg et al. argue, respresented 'the welding together of a nation of distrustful parts'. The colonies only entered into the confederation 'with the gravest of misgivings and then only with the assurance of the "limited state": a federal government thought sufficiently weak so as not to threaten their separate powers' (Gronbjerg et al., 1978, p. 14). It is still the case, they conclude, that, 'no group has trusted the other quite enough to allow for the development of a strong central government that might fall into the hands of another group' (p. 15). Thus the devolution of powers and responsibilities, the principle of 'States rights' and the abhorrence of central government have been long established. If, as Wilensky claims, a certain degree of political centralization is a prerequisite for the development of coherent social policies and pro-welfare attitudes this may begin to explain why America has followed a different path from many other industrialized countries.

However, there were conflicting trends, both prior to and after the establishment of the Federal Government which indicated that America would go the way of European countries such as England, France, Germany and Holland in establishing at least some level of public welfare provision. The early colonists were faced, from the very beginning, with the problem of how to deal with vagrancy and with the question of who should be responsible for the sick, the elderly and paupers. The obvious model was the Elizabethan Poor Law of 1601, and this was adopted, almost without modification, in most of the colonies. All the main features of the English system — the principle of local responsibility (introduced by the Law of Settlement, 1662), workhouses, outdoor relief for the 'deserving poor', 'liable relatives' clauses, the stigma of poverty and the condemnation of the poor as lazy, immoral and feckless — were present. Public authorities accepted, albeit very reluctantly, a degree of responsibility for the poor. In New England the town was the usual administrative body concerned with poor relief, while in the southern colonies it was the parish. The Plymouth colony, in 1642, was the first to provide poor relief financed through taxation, and many others subsequently followed.

Although some of the practices established in the early seventeenth century, were harsh and repressive it is important to note that the principle of State responsibility for the relief of the poor had nevertheless been accepted. As Mencher observed:

> It was a period of experimentation in welfare strategy supported by a climate of social responsibility combined with state interest. Both the principles and practices explored during this time have been significant for the whole of later welfare planning. (1967, p. 50)

By the end of the colonial period, therefore, two interwoven patterns of thought could be distinguished. On the one hand there was the resistance to the centralization of political functions and power and on the other there was a grudging acceptance of the need to make some public provision for those poor whose families were unable to care for them. Out of these two positions either strong anti- or pro-welfare attitudes might have developed. An excessive emphasis on the powers of local government and firm adherence to settlement laws and residence requirements for relief would have inhibited the development of a coherent, national welfare policy. Alternatively, the simple framework for poor relief established by the colonies might have become the basis for a more liberal and more extensive system of economic and social support with the State playing a central role. In fact, as we shall see, it was the anti-welfare position which assigned only a minimal role to the State which came to predominate.

The beliefs of the colonial period were gradually superseded by the doctrines of *laissez-faire*, the 'free market' and 'minimum government'. This was not a peculiarly American phenomenon and similar changes were felt in most of the countries of Europe. It was in America, however, that the tradition of *laissez-faire* became most firmly established and found its purest form. The commitment to individualism was almost total. As Mencher reported:

> Whatever the rationale, unfettered self-interest was the goal. Institutions of control, such as government, were essentially evil because they were restricting and represented a cultural lag. (1967, p. 63)

Reform of the poor laws (following the 1834 Poor Law Amendment Act in England) became a priority — not with a view to making them more humane but rather in order to reduce public expenditure by enhancing their deterrent effects. It was also argued that poor relief, especially outdoor relief, was harmful in creating a dependence upon public support and in offering no incentive for the pauper to become self-reliant. The main controversy centred upon the role of government in the provision of poor relief and the extent of public responsibility for the poor, especially the able-bodied or 'undeserving poor'. Thus far the development of social policy in America had followed a similar pattern to England and many other countries of Europe. There were obviously certain differences in social conditions, especially those experienced by the early colonists — the need to deal with large numbers of 'unattached' immigrants — and, later, during the Civil War the need to provide for soldiers, refugees and former slaves which gave rise to some modification of the European model of poor relief. However, by and large, by the end of the nineteenth century America had travelled a similar path to a similar destination, the principle of *laissez-faire* and minimum government intervention had been accepted. Considerable emphasis was placed upon the desirability of self-help and voluntary and charitable aid which would aim to make the pauper independent of public funds. The Charity Organization Society in America, as in Britain, was an important influence upon attitudes to social welfare and in the actual provision of services. The first branch of the COS was founded in Buffalo in 1877 and was closely modelled, in both spirit and goals, upon its English predecessors.

It was only in the early 1900s, when Britain, Germany and other countries were beginning to move out of the period of *laissez-faire* in social policy towards the acceptance of the desirability of limited public provision in the fields of health, housing, education and income maintenance, that America began to diverge from the common trend. By 1900 Germany had established the first compulsory, and contributory, social insurance schemes which provided both pensions and invalidity benefits, while Denmark and New Zealand had both introduced non-contributory pension schemes. Britain came a little later in 1908 and Holland in 1913 (Kaim-Caudle, 1973). Meanwhile, social policy in the United States was still inspired primarily by a belief in voluntarism and self-help. Although some States introduced benefits for widows, veterans, the blind and elderly, in the early 1900s, it was not until 1935 that the first Federal initiative, in the Social Security Act of that year, was seen. The State programmes were extremely limited in their coverage and the benefit levels they offered. They strictly enforced residence requirements and filial responsibility clauses. The main form of public provision in many States was the workhouse or poor farm and many of the deterrent aspects of poor law policy were still very much in evidence.

An account by Harry Evans in 1926, entitled *The American poor farm and its inmates* reported that:

> Dangerous insanitary conditions prevail at most poor farms. The rule is water from wells, outdoor, filthy privies, no sewerage or cesspools. Sanitation cannot be maintained among a group of feeble-minded paupers, huddled together, some of whom cannot care for their own bodies, practically all of them given to slovenly habits, without running water and sewerage. Slop and garbage are thrown out the kitchen door, or dumped in piles about the yard. The drain from the grounds and privies contaminates the well water. Often there is no hot water to wash bedding and clothing. (p. 13)

Evans attributed at least part of the problem to the fact that many of the poor farms were run by private entrepreneurs on a profitmaking basis. In certain States public auctions were held at which individuals would make bids to run the farms. Many other dubious practices were also reported. Children were apprenticed, auctioned off or simply shipped westwards and dumped in neighbouring States so that they would not become a drain on local resources. Little attempt was made to separate out the sick, elderly, women, children and criminal elements in the institutions and all were housed together. Some States deliberately sent convicted criminals to poor farms to serve out their sentences, rather than to prison, while in other States the traffic flowed in the opposite direction. In Terrel County, Georgia, for example, Evans discovered that:

> some years ago the increase in applications for county aid became so numerous that the county commissioners abandoned outdoor relief to the poor and adopted the plan of sending applicants to the convict farm, Since then there have been few applications. (p. 36)

Where the state did intervene it was primarily in the role of inspector and arbitrator and it did not meet with any notable success.

By 1930, therefore, America had become firmly established as one of the 'welfare state laggards'. Despite the introduction of social legislation in the 1930s (under the 'New Deal') and the 1960s (the 'War on Poverty'), and despite a substantial growth (in relative terms) in public expenditure in social welfare over the last fifteen years, it has maintained this position, well behind most other advanced, industrialized societies. The main exception is in the field of educational policy where America has been generally progressive and where the State has played a more decisive role than in other areas of the health and welfare services. Although estimates vary, most sources (ILO, 1972; OECD, 1976) indicate that the United States ranks behind many of the countries of Europe, as well as New Zealand, the USSR, Canada and Israel in the percentage of GNP spent, by the State, on social welfare. The position has been summarized by Anthony King when he wrote:

> In the United States, in short, the machinery of government is not an accepted piece of institutional apparatus to be made use of as and when required; it is a sort of emergency appliance to be wheeled out only in the most extreme circumstances and put back in its place, if possible, as soon as the emergency is over. (1973, p. 419)

How can we explain this? Why did America never really emerge, with any conviction, from the period of *laissez-faire*? Why, in the words of Wilensky and Lebeaux, has America been:

> more reluctant than any rich democratic country to make a welfare effort appropriate to its affluence. Our support of

> national welfare programmes is halting, our administration of services for the less privileged is mean. We move toward the welfare state but we do it with ill grace, carping and complaining all the way. (1965, p. xvii)

Why has the role of the State, as a provider of welfare, continued to be small, compared with other nations? Why did convergence in their social policies not occur to any significant degree? The answers, of course, are extremely complex and some of the possible explanations which have been advanced are less convincing than others. We can, however, test out some of our theories about the determinants of social policy, to see which might give us clues and possible 'leads'.

America, the reluctant welfare State: some explanations

If we begin by looking at social policy in America prior to, and including, the nineteenth century we can see that 'cultural diffusion' acted as a positive force for the development of social provision. The experiences of the early European colonists formed the basis for public programmes in the 'New World'. Many of the attitudes to the poor and to vagrants, and the principles on which poor relief were based, were a direct reflection of contemporary thinking in Europe. However, although 'cultural diffusion' resulted in the establishment of poor relief systems (some of which were generous and humane) a number of negative factors outweighed this influence and, over a period of years, inhibited the further development of social programmes in America, especially at the national level.

First of all *cultural and ethnic heterogeneity* appeared to work against the extension of the State (especially the Federal) role, in welfare. As Gronbjerg et al. observe, 'The ethnic, regional and racial groupings that make up American society have never much trusted one another and for that reason have been loath to put much power in one another's hands' (1978, p. 14). The consequence has been that, rather than supporting the State as provider of last resort, the American public have poured huge resources into private charities and into self-help groups. There is a wide, and probably unparalleled, range of organizations which provide for different ethnic and religious groups or groups with special needs, reflecting the considerable fragmentation of beliefs and allegiances in contemporary American society.

Related to this has been a confident and unswerving belief in the virtues of *laissez-faire, the free market* and *the capacity of economic growth to eliminate poverty* and deprivation. Some commentators have argued that this belief in *laissez-faire* was weakened, or even eradicated, by the impact of the Great Depression in the 1930s, when it was recognized that State intervention may be required to deal with the problems of mass unemployment. Rimlinger, for example, claims that:

> The 1930s was an important turning point in American economic history. The whole system of capitalist free enterprise was suddenly on the defensive on a scale never before witnessed in America. . . . In the 1930s the system built on individualistic foundations faltered and was failing in a world in which collectivisit methods were mastering, for the first time in history, the operation of industrial economies. (1971, pp. 193-4)

However, we might equally argue that the New Deal programmes introduced to deal with this crisis were really a 'hiccup' in the otherwise smooth progress of *laissez-faire* capitalism. Certainly, many of the programmes were designed to shore up the institutions of capitalism, such as the banks and certain businesses. As one commentator remarked, 'President Franklin Delano Roosevelt came not to bury capitalism but to restore it' (James, 1972, p. 50).

Other programmes (with the exception of most of the measures introduced under the 1935 Social Security Act) were abandoned once the immediate crisis had passed. A good deal of the evidence which has been used to support the view that the origins of the American 'welfare state' date from the Wall St crash in 1929 is certainly open to question. On the contrary, there are grounds for arguing that the supporters of *laissez-faire* and 'minimum government' then and now, have wielded considerably more power and influence than advocates of an increased State role in welfare. Indeed, Franklin Roosevelt — who is often credited with having set America on its road to the Welfare State — actually wrote to a friend in 1934 'What I am seeking is the abolition of relief altogether. I cannot say so out loud yet but I hope to be able to substitute work for relief' (quoted in Leuchtenburg, 1963, p. 124).

Tied in with these views about the desirability of non-interventionism are other *ideological factors* which have delayed the growth of public welfare in America. The so-called 'ideology of individualism' which has sustained the opponents of State welfare has, according to Feagin a number of components:

> 1. That each individual should work hard and strive to succeed in competition with others.
> 2. That those who work hard should be rewarded with success (seen as wealth, property, prestige and power).
> 3. That because of widespread and equal opportunity those who work hard will in fact be rewarded with success.
> 4. That economic failure is an individual's own fault and reveals lack of effort and other character defects. (1975, pp. 91–2)

Several studies, including a survey by Feagin himself, have shown how widely accepted this ideology of individualism appears to be in America (see James, 1972). There have been a number of effects on policy. Firstly, the notion of individual causation of social problems (or, 'blaming the victim' as Ryan (1971) has called it), means that solutions are often seen in terms of therapy or the rehabilitation of 'problem families' or individuals. It is believed that the provision of 'passive' welfare support in the form of income or services will only exacerbate the situation by making the individual more dependent upon external help. Education and training, in a variety of forms, are seen as the key to success. Another effect on policy has been the emphasis on creating opportunities for self-help set up by the Economic Opportunity Act in 1964. The net effect of these attitudes has been that:

> Public policy towards the poor has always borne the mark of America's adherence to the liberal tradition, with its emphasis on individualistic materialism and antagonism toward comprehensive social planning. (James, 1972, p. 49)

The *lack of centralization* of American governmental activities and the desire to preserve local autonomy and 'States' rights' have also worked against the development of uniform, national policies on welfare. They have engendered what Wilensky and Lebeaux have aptly named 'the tyranny of locality' (1965, p. xix). The result has been enormous regional inequalities in the provision of benefits and services. Although the Federal Government, since the 1960s, has contributed an increasing (and not insignificant) share of public expenditure on social welfare, the responsibility for raising revenue and allocating resources still rests primarily with State, county and city administrations. We have already attributed this, in part, to cultural and ethnic heterogeneity (Gronbjerg, 1978; Katznelson, 1978) and the unwillingness to delegate powers and duties to a distant and potentially uncontrollable central government. Wilensky and Lebeaux (1965) have argued that the resistance to centralization derives from the desire to preserve the free market and the belief that intervention of the Federal Government is only justified where it will strengthen the freedom of the market.

The effects of what they describe as 'the extreme jurisdictional fragmentation of the American political system' have also been discussed by Heidenheimer et al. (1976, pp. 97–101) and have been contrasted with those of many European countries:

> Just as local communities in the United States have resisted federal pressure to reorganise school systems so that available resources could be centrally collected and distributed within metropolitan regions, so they have consistently rejected proposals to create supra-local planning agencies that would have the authority to enforce zoning and transportation decisions. In contrast, European national governments have used their leverage both to promote reform at the local level and to mediate conflicts among local jurisdictions. (p. 98)

The fiercest debates, about local control have centred upon educational policies. There has been an increase in Federal directives and resources in recent years, both with respect to the desegregation of schools and the provision of subsidies through the Elementary and Secondary Education Act (1965) and Project Head Start (1965).

At the same time, there has also been change in the opposite direction, a devolution of responsibility to local school boards. However, increasing Federal intervention in education has not resulted in a uniform system. As Heidenheimer et al. explain:

> National leaders who attempt to formulate policy at the local level must deal with an array of state and local units holding sufficient power to veto or at least offer firm resistance to national initiatives. (1976, p. 101)

This was particularly obvious in the 1950s when many of the Southern States evaded the responsibility to desegregate placed upon them by a Supreme Court ruling, by a variety of ingenious and rather suspect techniques. Ironically, when the position changed in the 1960s and the Southern States were making rapid strides towards desegregation, increasing segregation in urban, school districts in the North was becoming apparent. It is clear, therefore, that the lack of centralization in many policy areas has inhibited the development of national social policies.

If, as Wilensky argues, another important determinant of the level and sophistication of social policy development is the *age of the system* we might not be surprised to find that the United States continued to lag behind Europe. Compared with Denmark, France, Germany, Italy, the Netherlands, Sweden and the United Kingdom, the United States was the last to provide compensation for injury at work (in 1908), the last to provide unemployment, invalidity, old age and survivors' benefits (in 1935), the last to provide sickness and maternity benefits (and even then only in a very limited national health programme in 1965) and, unlike all the other countries, still has no system of family allowances. However, although information about the age of the system may help us to account for the particular stage which a country's development has reached, it does not necessarily tell us anything about the role of the State in that system. Generally speaking, we might argue that the older the system the greater the role of the State (although there are exceptions to this proposition — notably Russia which only began to develop its contemporary services in 1917 and where the State role is now very extensive), but it is an imprecise relationship and a variable of dubious validity.

A more important determinant in the case of America would be the *low level of unionization* and the relative weakness, ineffectiveness and antipathy of working-class and trade union movements in the field of social reform. Union membership in America is currently less than 22 per cent of the workforce and declining (see Social Indicators, 1976) whereas membership in Britain is around 52 per cent and increasing (Social Trends, 1979). Historically American trade unions have tended to oppose rather than support proposed extensions in public welfare programmes and increased government intervention. Heidenheimer et al. show that, at the turn of the century, when there was some pressure for the introduction of social insurance:

> Leaders of unions were particularly opposed to sickness and unemployment insurance, largely for fear of weakening union influence over workers and increasing workers' dependence on government — labour's leaders decried social insurance as contrary to American traditions of self-help and feared interference with the unions' own relationship with workers. Gradually, eco-

> nomic pressures led to changes in some of these views, but American labor unions generally remained more an obstacle than a creative force in income support policy. (1976, pp. 196–7)

As far as working-class movements are concerned Piven and Cloward (1977) have argued that, although they sometimes succeed in achieving reform, they have very often failed. This is so because the institutions of American society have been particularly successful in securing their 'political docility' (p.7) and in limiting their opportunities 'to press for their own class interests'. They refer to Edelman's observation that:

> The American poor have required less coercion and less in social security guarantees to maintain their quiescence than has been true in other developed countries, even authoritarian ones like Germany and notably poor ones like Italy; for the guilt and self-concepts of the poor have kept them docile. (1971, p. 56)

The research conducted by James (1972) and Feagin (1975) would also tend to support the view that the ideology of individualism has been so successful in lowering the self-esteem of the poor that they have with some exceptions, been quiescent rather than agitating for social reform. Clearly there have been outbursts of discontent which have resulted in some concessions in the form of improved welfare provision but protest has not been sustained. This can be explained, in part, by the relative fragmentation of class and political allegiances and the absence of any socialist or social democratic party which could act as the political vehicle for maintaining the momentum of reform movements. Conversely the high percentage of votes for the Republican party (48.02%) as compared with right-wing voting patterns in other countries (Belgium, 16.02%; Denmark, 18.76%; France, 35.15%; Germany, 45.97%; Sweden, 14.84%; United Kingdom, 45.27%) may be another factor which explains the continuing popular antipathy towards public welfare (Castles and Mckinlay, 1979).

Finally, the hostility and considerable strength of *pressure groups private and business interests* and *professional organizations* has seriously impeded the progress of social welfare reform. This is particularly apparent in the field of medical care where the American Medical Association has consistently fought the introduction of national health insurance since the first bill introduced in Congress in 1912. The AMA has been singularly effective and remains a powerful force against change. Similarly, the private health insurance companies who currently finance the majority of medical expenses have also opposed any moves to introduce a national insurance scheme, as have various consumer groups who fear the loss of choice, individual freedom and 'creeping socialism' which any such system might entail. The so-called 'tax payers' revolts' in 1978, which led several State governments to reduce taxation, and thereby, the resources available for public expenditure on welfare activities, have also limited the development of social policies.

Many of the determinants of social policy which we described in the first section of this chapter prove, therefore, to be of some significance when we attempt to explain why the role of the State in American welfare systems should be so limited. In each case a good deal more research is required to elucidate the precise relationship between the social, economic and political factors we have enumerated, and State involvement in welfare. However, a broad picture emerges from the data which is already assembled. We can see that certain hypotheses do not seem to be supported by the evidence, for example Wilensky's proposition that the level of economic development is the key determinant of social policy. America has had a high rate of economic growth, a high per capita GNP and considerably more resources which might have been directed towards social welfare than most comparable countries. It may be that a high level of economic development is a necessary condition for the development of national social policies but it is clearly not a sufficient condition and we would still need to explain, therefore, why America has not chosen to devote a large proportion of its income to social welfare programmes.

We can also see, from the above discussion, that the role of the State is both an important influence on social policy and is, itself, determined by a wide range of influences. The interrelationships between the different variables which shape social policies are obviously very complex and can only be disentangled with care and with more detailed investigation than the 'macro' approach, followed here, actually permits. The American system of welfare is a good example of the 'residual model of welfare' which we described in chapter 3. It accords a relatively limited role to the State, which is regarded as a provider of last resort. There is a large private sector in welfare; benefit levels in the public sector are low and coverage is minimal. Many services are strictly means-tested, are punitive and designed to deter 'undeserving' applicants. A number of factors account for this attitude towards social policy and the role of the State and we have pointed to some of them. The position might best be summarized as follows:

> the state plays a more limited role in America than elsewhere because Americans, more than other people, want it to play a limited role. . . . The pattern of American policy is what it is, not because . . . the demands made on government are different from those made in other countries . . . but rather because Americans believe things that other people do not believe and make assumptions that other people do not make. (King, 1973, p. 423)

Finally, the implication in this section has been that — while America is doing things one way — other countries are doing them differently. We turn now to a brief consideration of the alternatives and to societies in which the role of the State is considerably greater than in America.

The role of the State: some alternatives

Most of the comparisons we have made above have been with the role of the State in European countries. In the case of Britain, France, Germany and others the part played by the State as a provider of welfare has consistently been greater than that in the United States, even in recent years when government intervention in the latter has been growing rapidly. The reasons for the growth of State welfare in European countries are not uniform and cannot simply be attributed to 'creeping socialism' or to the inevitable convergence of industrial societies. Both the origins of and patterns of development have differed quite significantly from one country or another. In the case of Germany, for example:

> the Governments which established or perpetuated State enterprises in the nineteenth century, especially in the 1870s and 1880s, were conservative in orientation and it was an imaginative conservative, Bismarck, who created the German system of social insurance; health insurance in 1883, old-age and invalidity insurance in 1889. (King, 1973, p. 310)

In France, public welfare systems have been developed on an *ad hoc* basis, often alongside private schemes and have been introduced (as in Britain) by governments of different political persuasions.

In all the European countries the State does have an important role in social policy but the evolution of that role, and the particular form it takes, varies. The most obvious contrast with the United States, however, is not illustrated by the case of Western Europe (although the differences are striking enough) but by socialist societies such as Russia, China, Cuba and the countries of Eastern Europe.

As Mishra has observed, in the ideal-type socialist society, State responsibility for meeting needs is 'total', benefits are distributed primarily on the basis of 'need', rather than ability to pay; the range and coverage of services is comprehensive and the role of non-statutory agencies is marginal (1977, p. 123). Obviously, socialist societies conform to the model to varying degrees but in most cases, at least, some of these features are evident.

In the Soviet Union, for example, the State is the main provider of services such as education, medical care and housing. Services are not totally free of charge, nor fully comprehensive, and private ownership of housing (approximately one-third of the market) is accepted. Even so the principle of State responsibility is fully acknowledged. It is reflected in many of the documents of the Communist Party and, in practice, in most areas of the social services. According to Madison, for example:

> The Soviets took a firm stand in favour of the 'institutional' approach to social welfare, thereby rejecting the 'residual' concept that was dominant before the Revolution. They did not think of welfare assistance as a sporadic activity to be brought into play only in cases of social breakdown, when the 'normal' market economy and/or family solicitude proved inadequate. (Madison, 1968, p. 49)

In 1917, when the Revolution took place, Russia was a long way behind its Western European counterparts in terms of social provision. It had taken longer to rid itself of punitive poor laws (and the system which sustained them) and to begin to construct more appropriate alternatives. Since then considerable progress has been made in filling the gaps in services and in establishing the right to social welfare as one of the principle rights of citizenship. This development has now been realized to the extent that a recent commentator on the medical care system in Russia can write:

> Given the ideological basis of the Soviet state, it is hardly necessary to make the point that the USSR contains no health care facilities provided by private owners or by religious and

philanthropic organizations, such as coexist with the British health service. (M. Ryan, 1978, p. 8)

The role of the State, as expressed in the 1961 Programme of the Communist party of the Soviet Union, is unequivocal, 'The socialist state is the only state which undertakes to protect and continuously improve the health of the whole population' (quoted in M. Ryan, 1978, p. 5).

Rimlinger (1971) has illustrated the ways in which the Communist Party envisages the relationship between the State and the citizen with respect to social policy. The virtual abolition of private ownership in most sections of the economy since 1917 has meant that considerably more responsibilities and power are vested in the institutions of government than is ordinarily the case in capitalist free-market economies. Unlike America and the countries of Western Europe the payment of benefits is not contingent upon contribution records or upon a contractual relationship between the government and the citizen. On the contrary, 'Soviet ideology stressed that social security benefits are a gift from the state — a genuine act of governmental benevolence, a true manifestation of socialist humanism (Rimlinger, 1971, p. 254).

The principles on which contemporary Russian social policy is based, therefore, are — in essence — in direct contrast with those of American social policy. However, although these two countries may be at opposite ends of a continuum in terms of the role accorded to the State we can see that they do not fit neatly into the 'residual' and 'institutional' models of welfare outline in chapter 3.

In practice, there are areas in which State intervention in America has occurred. Since 1965 there have been limited Federal programmes of health care for the elderly (Medicare) and the poor (Medicaid). There is a certain amount of public housing, although it is only a tiny percentage of the total market (around 2 per cent) and there are Federal benefits for the elderly, widows, veterans, the disabled and for dependent children. The most striking deviation from the 'residual' model is in the case of education policy. Public expenditure on education is now more than five times as much as private expenditure. The Federal government is responsible for a small proportion of these costs and the rest are borne by State and local governments. Although America may lag behind European countries in most other respects it is one of the leaders in the education field. It has a higher proportion of children in full-time education after the age of 19 than France, West Germany, Italy, the Netherlands, Norway, Sweden and the United Kingdom, it has a higher per capita expenditure per pupil than all these countries except Sweden and spends a higher percentage of GNP on public education than all except the Netherlands.

Russia, similarly, deviates from the 'institutional' model in a number of respects. First of all, there are areas in which private ownership and control is evident, particularly in housing (see Mishra, 1977, p. 139). At the same time, the ideal of comprehensive benefits was nowhere near achievement until 1965 when social security programmes were extended to cover the collective farm workers who had originally been excluded. Any semblance of equality of treatment in income maintenance programmes has been rather a long time in coming and until the reforms of 1956 benefits were closely tied to prior earnings and were of a regressive nature (Madison, 1973, p. 99). Inequalities are also evident in the provision of medical care. There are distinct regional variations in doctor:patient ratios, preferential treatment for certain occupational groups, Party members and members of the government and charges are made, selectively, for drugs, and dental and opthalmic services (M. Ryan, 1978).

We can see, from these brief examples, that the question we should be asking is not 'does the State have a role in the provision of social welfare?' but 'what role does it have?' and 'how is that role determined?' Even in countries such as America, where the extent of State involvement, overall, is low we can see that its influence may be very significant, in both positive and negative ways. It is also necessary to recognize that a macro approach to the analysis of determinants of social policy may result in caricatures of countries and their social policies which omit important details. It is reasonable enough to argue that, generally speaking, America is a good example of a country in which the role of the State in social policy is low and Russia typifies a country in which it is high. However, the caveats which we noted above are important and there is no substitute for detailed analysis once ideal types and general guidelines have been established.

The purpose of this chapter has been to show that the determinants of social policy (of which the role of the State is only one) weave an intricate web which may often be difficult to penetrate. However, the various studies referred to above have indicated a number of leads which may be followed in establishing which particular influences have governed the shape and character of social policy in different societies. The student's task is to use these general principles to explore and explain the origins and outcomes of social policy in the country or countries with which he/she is concerned.

CHAPTER 5

Determinants of Social Policy II: The Role of Religion

The influence of religious ideas and practice upon social policy has been of considerable significance, and different religious beliefs have resulted in a wide variety of policy responses. As R.H. Tawney observed in 1926, there are, 'perhaps four main attitudes which religious opinion may adopt toward the world of social institutions and economic relations' (1966 ed. p. 30). It may regard them as questions from which man could, and should, escape, for the good of his soul. It may regard them as 'matters of indifference, belonging to a world with which religion has no concern.' It may actively pursue social reform 'for the removal of some crying scandal' or it may accept social inequalities and degradation 'as the squalid scaffolding from amid which the life of the spirit must rise'. Each of these positions can be discerned in contemporary social policy in different societies. In some contexts the Church has carefully cultivated a non-interventionist stance, in others it has been crusading and reformist, while in others it has maintained that the true path to salvation is through the relief of suffering and hardship.

Religious doctrine has been as a source of criticism and a source of legitimacy of social and economic inequality. While some have argued that Christian doctrine should be interpreted as demanding humane and equal treatment for all God's children others have argued that inequalities are, in fact, God-given and serve a useful purpose. In this case, therefore, it is not the proper function of the Christian to intervene (other than in a very marginal, palliative role) in a system which God has ordained. The organic analogy is employed to show that different social classes perform unequal but essential functions in the maintenance of the social system, just as every organ contributes to the efficient functioning of the human body. As Tawney put it, the belief is that:

> Between classes there must be inequality; for otherwise a class cannot perform its function, or — a strange thought to us — enjoy its rights. Peasants must not encroach on those above them. Lords must not despoil peasants. Craftsmen and merchants must receive what will maintain them in their calling and no more. As a rule of social policy, the doctrine was at once repressive and protective (1966, p. 36).

There are areas of policy in which the Church has adopted a well-defined position and the influence of religious ideas is clearly discernible. For example, the Catholic Church has traditionally opposed divorce, abortion and contraception — practices which, if not actively encouraged by other religious and secular institutions, are at least tolerated. Similarly we can trace direct links between the growth of social welfare in nineteenth-century Britain, especially in the voluntary sector, and ideas about Christian responsibilities and duties and the nature of Christian fellowship. Many contemporary social services in fact originated in the activities of religious groups in the nineteenth century and earlier. We have also indicated, in chapter 3, the importance of Christian belief and the 'social conscience thesis' on the ways in which social problems came to be perceived, and the kind of solutions which were considered appropriate. In other societies, such as Eire, the debate about religion and social policy has centred upon the proper relationship between the Church and the State and the State has generally been reluctant to intervene in social welfare matters which are considered to be largely the preserve of the Church and the family. In other situations, however, the influence of religion has been much less direct, and is only one of a range of factors which have governed the ways in which social policies have evolved.

There are, essentially, two aspects to the relationship between religion and social policy. Firstly, there is the influence of religious ideas and beliefs on social policy and, secondly, there is the role of the Church as a provider of welfare. In practice, of course, these two are often closely interrelated. The purpose of this chapter is to show how the comparative analysis of the influence of religion, both historically and cross-nationally, may highlight a series of important determinants of social policy. We also use the broad comparative approach to explore the hypothesis that the secularization of social policy (in which the State gradually takes over the main welfare functions of the Church) follows on from industrialization and urbanization in most countries in which public welfare systems have been developed.

The influence of religious ideas

The influence of religious beliefs, not only amongst the Christian religions but in Buddhism, Judaism and others, cannot be over-emphasized. Religious doctrine has established the rationale for many social welfare activities and to the extent that there is an ideology of social policy in different societies it has often provided it. The influence of religious ideas was especially felt in pre-industrial societies and where Church rather than State was the main source of teaching. As the institutions of government began to take over such functions as the relief of the poor and education the Church frequently acted as a conservative force arguing that State intervention was both morally wrong and practically inappropriate. A few illustrations may serve to indicate the diversity and extent of religious influences upon social policy.

Although we may readily relate the philosophy of social policy in Western Europe and America to Judaeo-Christian beliefs some research suggests that the impact of religion is felt more widely.

Many aspects of social work and social policy in Japan have clearly been shaped by the teachings of Buddhism with its emphasis on the virtues of 'thoughtfulness, sympathy, gentleness, kindness, mercy, pity and benevolence' (Sugimoto, 1968, p. 4.) It is said that Buddha himself, Guatama Siddhartha, established institutions for the care of the sick and the poor and provided shelter for travellers. However, the credit for first organizing charitable work on any scale is attributed to Prince Regent Shotoku in the fifth century BC who built four famous institutions know as The Home of the Merciful Rice Field, the Home of the Venerable Rice Field, the Home for Treatment of Diseases and the Medical Almshouse (Sugimoto, 1968, p. 5.) According to Sugimoto:

> The establishment of these four institutions characterized the later development of social work in Japan so that relief of the poor and care for the sick became closely tied with the educational and religious work of enlightenment and ethical teachings based on Buddhism. Shotoku also set the pattern of the close

> relationship of government, religion and social work which has been maintained in varying degrees throughout Japanese history. (1968, p. 5)

Later, in the eighth century, the records show the Buddhists had begun to establish orphanages and homes for the blind. The motivation for building orphanages is said to have arisen from the story of Kishibojin, the guardian deity of children.

> Kishibojin was a devil who enjoyed eating children. In order to punish her, Buddha hid the child of Kishibojin, which made her realize the sorrow of the mothers whose children she had eaten. She finally became a follower of Buddha and was made the guardian deity of children.

This story was used to teach that children were just as important as adults and needed to be protected from hazard and misfortunes so that they could develop their potential.

The advent of Christianity in the mid-nineteenth century meant the introduction of more advanced medical care and the building of hospitals and schools. To some extent the work of Buddhist reformers was overshadowed by the more efficient methods and better organization of the Christian missionaries. By 1900 government responsibility for certain welfare activities was beginning to be accepted and Buddhists began to reassert themselves in the private sector establishing voluntary organizations for the elderly, for children and for prisoners. Although the influence of Buddhism may be said to have declined in the post-industrial period it is still estimated that '70% of the social work in Japan is under religious auspices' (Sugimoto, 1968, p. 8).

We can see, from this brief example, that religious beliefs in Japan had very different origins and manifestations from those in the West. Even so the policy outcomes were similar. The first type of support took the form of institutional care, especially for the poor and the sick, and specialized services for the elderly, for the blind and for children developed later. Subsequently, many of these functions were taken over by the State and religious groups were left to find a role for themselves in the non-State sector of social policy.

In other contexts the religious beliefs of individual social reformers can also be shown to have had an important influence on the development of social policy. As Asa Briggs points out:

> It is not without interest that Lohmann who had advised Bismarck and went on to advise William II in the formulation of the far-reaching Labour Code of 1891, was a deeply religious man, the son of a Westphalian Lutheran pastor. Canon W.L. Blackley (1830-1902), the pioneer of old age pensions schemes not only in Britain but in other parts of the world and the founder of the National Providence League, was an honorary canon of Winchester Cathedral. On the Liberal side — and there was a close association in Britain between religious non-conformity and political liberalism — Seebohm Rowntree (1871–1954), one of the first systematic investigators of the facts of poverty was a Quaker. The whole attack on the limitations of the poor law was guided though not exclusively, by men of strong religious principles (1961, p. 251)

The religious teachings of Catholicism have also, as we illustrate in the next section, influenced social policy, especially in countries in which Catholicism is the dominant religion and, as Briggs suggests:

> Papal encyclicals, notably Rerum Novarum (1891), were not only manifestos in crusades against liberalism or socialism but were also important documents in the evolution of Sozialpolitik. (1961, p. 250)

The case of Eire

If we take the case of Eire we can see that the influence of religious beliefs has also had a profound and lasting impact upon the organization of the whole of contemporary society, not only in the field of social policy. In a country in which approximately 95 per cent of the population are members of the same religion (Catholicism) it is hardly surprising that the impact of the Church has been strongly felt.

Until partition in 1922 social policy in Ireland had developed along similar lines to that in England. The Poor Relief (Ireland) Act of 1838 had provided for a poor law system closely modelled on that established in England in 1834. Before this date any welfare provisions which did exist had developed on an *ad hoc* basis and had actually been organized by parishes. During the previous century a number of workhouses had been built but the regimes were harsh and punitive, and designed primarily to suppress begging. However, facilities were not extensive and a Commission on the Poor Laws in 1833 discovered that there were only nine workhouses in the whole country (Farley, 1964, p 1). The administration of the Poor Law in Ireland closely followed the English pattern — with the establishment of 'unions', Board of Guardians, the operation of the 'workhouse test' and the principle of 'less eligibility' and within ten years of 1838 some 130 workhouses were built. The widespread distress engendered by the failure of the potato crop in 1845 gave rise to a second piece of legislation — The Poor Relief (Ireland) Act of 1847 — which for the first time allowed the provision of outdoor relief. Nevertheless (unlike the English system) the Irish Poor Law relied primarily on 'indoor relief' and it was not until the 1920s when workhouses were either closed down or converted for other purposes, that 'outdoor relief' was generally given. When the Irish Free State was established in 1922 the Irish government took over the administration of the existing social security programmes (old age pensions, national health insurance and unemployment insurance) previously administered from England, as well as the Poor Law.

Although the Constitution of the Irish Free State (1922) reflected a number of beliefs about the relationship between the Church, the State and social policy it was not until the passage of the Constitution of Ireland in 1937 which Mansergh describes as 'new from top to bottom' and 'unquestionably indigenous in character' (1958, p. 284) that their full implications became apparent. As Basil Chubb remarked:

> The Constitution, while obviously in the liberal democratic tradition and influenced by its predecessors is also markedly Christian, and more particularly Roman Catholic, in tone, language and content. Articles 41 and 42 which deal with the family and education contain a clear and unequivocal enunciation of Catholic principles. (Chubb, 1963, pp. 20-1, 34)

Article 41 declares that 'the State recognizes the Family as the natural primary and fundamental unit group of society, and as a moral institution possessing inalienable and imprescriptible rights, antecedent and superior to all positive law.'

Its purpose, therefore, is to protect the institution of marriage, and the dissolution of marriage, by divorce, is forbidden. The special position of women within the family is also discussed and the Constitution establishes that a mother's rightful place is in the home.

> the State shall, therefore, endeavour to ensure that mothers shall not be obliged by economic necessity to engage in labour to the neglect of their duties in the home. (Article 41)

Article 42, which is concerned with education, declares that the family is 'the primary and natural educator' and that, while parents have both the right and duty to educate their children, they are free to decide whether this education will take place at home or in school. The State, however, has the obligation to ensure that every child receives 'a certain minimum education' and, where parents do not fulfill their responsibilities, the State 'as guardian of the common good' may do so.

Article 43, in accordance with Catholic teaching, establishes 'the right to the private ownership of external goods' while Article 44, although emphasizing 'the special position of the Holy Catholic Apostolic and Roman Church as the guardian of the Faith professed by the great majority of the citizens' guarantees freedom of profession and practice of religion.

Article 45, which is entitled 'Directive Principles of Social Policy is again 'largely based on Catholic teaching and couched in Catholic terms' (Chubb, 1963, p. 38). Citizens are encouraged to provide for their needs 'through their occupations' rather than seeking external support. The State, however, undertakes to provide for 'the weaker in the community', especially women and children. Concentration of ownership and wealth is condemned and the State is empowered to protect the citizens against 'unjust exploitation'. Finally, Article 45 recommends that 'there may be established on the land in economic security as many families as practicable'.

The pursuit of religious beliefs and principles, especially with respect to social policy, is unusually explicit, therefore, in the Constitution of Ireland. We can now turn to look, in more detail, at the teachings of Catholicism and examine how, in practice, the influence of religion on social policy has been felt. The main features of Catholic belief, many of which are reflected in the Constitution, are as follows.

Firstly, the family is recognized as being the most important social unit and one which both Church and State should seek to protect and preserve. The papal encyclical *Rerum Novarum* (1891) in which Pope Leo XIII emphasized the independence of the family from the State, set the tone for much of the Church's teaching. Its sentiments are repeated in Monsignor Parkinson's *A Primer of Social Science* which was widely used as a 'textbook' of Catholicism:

> The family is the primary product of nature, and is self-contained. Into the family the State has no right of entry except to maintain rights not otherwise defensible. The children, until they grow up belong to the parents, as being a part and a continuation of themselves. The parents are the natural and primary educators of their offspring, with which they are united by the strongest ties of affection. (p. 26)

The result has been an emphasis on the need to develop social policies with a family, group and community focus. Catholic social policies, in principle therefore, are imbued with none of the fierce individualism characteristic of those policies proposed by Protestant and other groups (although it should be noted that, in actual practice, the outcomes may be almost indistinguishable). Catholics also advocated the development of Church-based welfare institutions as against those of the State.

Secondly, there has been an emphasis, in Catholic teaching, on the desirabilty of the widespread ownership of property. It was envisaged that, in the ideal society, every man would own and work his own land and that the concentration of ownership in the hands of a few would be eliminated. For those who could not provide for themselves and their families in this way a third principle of Catholic teaching — the notion of the 'just wage' — was invoked. The 'just wage' was intended to be a reflection of the market value of a man's contribution to his community, and an allowance for meeting those needs which were consonant with his social status.

Related to these ideas was the fourth and rather complex principle of 'subsidiary function' or 'subsidiarity'. This maintained that different social groupings and classes should co-operate, without the need of State intervention, to create an effective and compassionate society. Although the notion of 'subsidiarity' had featured in Catholic teaching since the twelfth century, contemporary usage of the term is normally attributed to the papal encyclical *Quadragesimo Anno* in 1931. This proposed that:

> just as it is wrong to withdraw from the individual and commit to the community at large what private enterprise and endeavour

> can accomplish, so it is likewise unjust and a gravely harmful disturbance of right order to turn over to a greater society of higher rank, functions and services which can be performed by lesser bodies on a lower plane. (quoted in Leaper, 1975, p. 83)

It is clear that such a position allows little scope for the State or for government institutions as providers of welfare. Coman has elaborated this point:

> In Catholic thought individuals, families and larger groups such as guilds or unions and professional or business associations should all co-operate harmoniously to form a society which would be an organic whole. The state's role would be that of supervision, assistance in the harmonisation of group interests, filling the gaps in voluntary provision and itself performing those functions which only the state could effectively undertake, e.g. internal law and order and defence against external enemies. It was hoped that spontaneous co-operation by the variety of groups within society would reduce the coercive intervention of the state to a minimum. (1977, p. 27)

Although Leaper maintains that the principle of subsidiarity was 'well-known, most respected and carefully studied' he also claims that 'it was almost completely ignored in practice, in Ireland and several other European countries' (Leaper, 1975, p. 82). However, Coman has shown that where the political and religious environment is favourable, as in Eire, the principle of subsidiarity can have significant practical outcomes. The most frequently quoted example of the strength of feeling about 'subsidiarity' is the case of the Mother and Child Health Bill in 1950. The proposals for a national health scheme for mothers and children were drawn up by Dr Noel Browne who was then Minister of Health. They included a recommendation that universal and free health education and medical care should be provided, by dispensary doctors, for all women and their children until the age of 16 years. The main aim of the service was to reduce the unacceptably high mortality rates of these groups. As in most countries where attempts have been made to introduce free, public health care there was strong opposition from doctors and their professional representatives. However, a far more serious (and effective) attack was launched by the Catholic bishops. In a letter to John Costello, the Prime Minister, the Bishop of Ferns, Dr Staunton (Secretary to the Hierarchy) argued that although the Bishops favoured the desire to improve public health:

> they feel bound by their office to consider whether the proposals are in accordance with Catholic moral teaching. In their opinion the powers taken by the state in the proposed Mother and Child Health Service are in direct opposition to the rights of the family and of the individual and are liable to very great abuse. . . .
> If adopted in law they would constitute a ready-made instrument for future totalitarian aggression. The right to provide for the health of children belongs to parents not to the State. The State has the right to intervene only in a subsidiary capacity, to supplement, not to supplant. (quoted in Coman, 1977, p. 96)

The letter went on to argue that a universal system which would take away the rights of all parents was unjustified if it was designed simply to protect a small minority 'from the so-called indignity of the means test'. Their main concern, however, was that the State would assume a responsibility for health education and for 'instruction in sex relations, chastity and marriage' which, they claimed, was strictly the preserve of the Church. They regarded, 'with the greatest apprehension' the suggestion that doctors would have 'the right to tell Catholic girls and women how they should behave in regard to this sphere of conduct at once so delicate and sacred'.

Eventually opposition to the scheme (led by the Catholic bishops) was so strong that is was withdrawn and Dr Browne actually resigned from office. A more limited scheme, which omitted the provision for health education, was subsequently enacted, in 1953, but as Coman concludes:

> It does, however, remain a striking fact that the Catholic bishops in Ireland, acting on a rigorous and in some ways a narrow interpretation of Catholic social policy had succeeded in largely causing the withdrawal of the Health Service Bill. (1977, p. 98)

The influence of the Church has also been felt in other areas of social policy, especially in education, where control of many primary and secondary schools still rests with the clergy. As Whyte has observed:

> Irish education is not merely denominationally controlled: it is clerically controlled . . . local control rests not with an elected

board, but with a single officer, the school manager, who in the case of a Catholic school is usually the parish priest. Secondary schools are equally free from elected local control. A minority of Catholic secondary schools are owned by laymen, but most are owned by dioceses or religious orders. The only schools in Ireland run by local authorities are technical or, as they were renamed in 1930, vocational schools. (1971, pp. 17-18)

It is probably in the area of family policy, however, where the role of the Church is most controversial. It is alleged that social workers are inhibited by Article 41 of the Constitution from protecting children in their own home, or, indeed outside it (see *The Guardian*, 13.9.79) and that the emphasis on the sanctity of the family, and subsidiarity of the State, seriously limits the help which can be given. The teachings of the Church with respect to contraception and abortion also affect the demographic structure of the population (resulting in high birth and fertility rates) which in turn creates the need for services such as maternity, child health and educational provision. Although the limited distribution of contraceptives was approved by the Irish government in August 1979 there has been some delay in implementing the legislation because of the reluctance of chemists to operate the scheme, and condoms are only available on doctors' prescriptions.

Further recent developments are slowly beginning to undermine the influence of the Church. An important test case was fought in the European Court of Human Rights in Strasbourg which ruled in October 1979 that the Irish Government was in breach of two articles of the European convention of human rights — article 6 which allows all citizens access to the courts and article 8 which protects family life. The case was brought by Mrs Josie Airey a market stallholder from Cork. She claimed that the Irish courts would not protect her from her violent estranged husband. The court would only issue an 'injunction' against him if a judicial separation was in force. The cost of procuring a judicial separation in the High Court however was beyond the means of Mrs Airey and she had been refused legal aid. Her case, therefore, was that she was unable to obtain justice because the High Court was open only to the rich. As a result of her successful appeal to the European Court the Irish government has now made some provision for the granting of three-month injunctions in the district courts.

Certain other discriminatory practices which may partially be attributed to the effects of Catholic teaching on the family have gradually been amended in the 1970s. The 'marriage bar', for example, which meant that women had to leave employment on their marriage, has largely been repealed. Equal pay legislation has been implemented and unmarried mothers and their children are treated, under income maintenance provisions, in the same way as other categories of one-parent families. Other recommendations, such as the development of day care facilities for the children of working mothers, have not, however been implemented and the notion that 'a woman's place is in the home' has not entirely been removed.

It would seem that a series of factors, since the early 1960s, have contributed to the decline of the influence of the Church on social policy. From this period public expenditure on health, social security and welfare has grown at a moderate rate while that on secondary and higher education has grown substantially. Overall, public expenditure has almost doubled, since 1960, as a percentage of GNP. Membership of the European Economic Community has brought a number of changes, one of which has been the move towards equal pay. There have also been more resources available, through the EEC, for social programmes and for experiments in welfare rights and anti-poverty projects. The establishment of the National Economic and Social Council in 1974 was part of a move towards social planning. One of the first actions of the Council was to commission a report, by David Donnison, which set out the criteria which might be used to determine a national 'approach to social policy'. One of the difficulties, at that time, was that there were few statistics available to help in the assessment of needs and demand for welfare. Subsequent reports were concerned to collect basic data and to devise concrete proposals for reform. Important changes have taken place, therefore, despite the continuing conservatism of some of the Catholic hierarchy with respect to social policy.

However, it should also be said that there have been changes within the Church itself during this period which have facilitated reform. In the papal encyclical *Mater et Magistra* (1961), for example, Pope John XXIII expressed his approval of the principle of social insurance.

> It is also true that more and more people today, through belonging to insurance and systems of social security find that they can face the future with the sort of confidence which formerly re-

> sulted from their possession of a certain amount of property. (Para. 10)

There has also been a certain liberalization of the Church's attitude on contraception, marriage to non-Catholics, divorce and the position of women. As Coman has remarked, there was a growing acceptance among Catholics in the 1960s (in England at least) that increasing State intervention in social policy was a 'fait accompli' (1977, p. 72). Some members of the English hierarchy have even welcomed the extension of public welfare facilities. Cardinal Heenan's pastoral letter in 1964, for example, argued that Catholics should, 'press politicians to hasten measures to bring relief to the old, the bereaved and the homeless' (quoted in Coman, 1977, p. 74).

In Ireland, with growing industrialization and urbanization, the teachings of the Catholic Church with respect to private ownership, the 'just wage', the economic role of women and subsidiarity became increasingly difficult to implement in the changing socio-economic conditions. Thus Catholic beliefs have become only one influence upon the direction in which social policy develops where, once, they were the key determinant of change (or the lack of it). Even acknowledging the decreasing significance of religion, however, it is difficult to concur entirely with Kaim-Caudle's assertion that:

> Social policy in the years ahead is not likely to be influenced by ideological, religious or moral considerations any more than it has been in the past. It does, however, seem probable that it will be shaped to an increasing extent by the general national aspirations of the population. (1967, p. 103)

A number of general points emerge from this discussion about the influence of religious ideas on social policy in Eire. First of all, Eire is a rather extreme case and there are few other countries in the West in which 95 per cent of the population are members of the same religious group. One would expect, therefore, that the importance of the religious influence would be felt more strongly here than in most other societies. Secondly, in societies with a plurality of religious beliefs the effects of one particular religion may be 'cancelled out' by the effects of others so that the overall impact on policy is relatively small. Even where 'separation' may originally encourage the development of strong religious sub-cultures within societies their influence may not be sustained and may be dissipated by extraneous socio-economic factors. Thirdly, when we discuss the role of different determinants of social policy we must understand that these roles are not fixed and do change over time. Thus, we can see that the influence of the Catholic Church in Eire, though still strong, may be diminishing as other determinants increase in importance. Fourthly, for religious influences to determine the development of social policy other political and social conditions must be favourable. Coman has illustrated this point and his conclusions are as follows:

> A comparative study of social developments in the French Fourth Republic, the Irish Republic and the United Kingdom in the decade after the Second World War seems to indicate that, in both its interpretation and application, Catholic social policy was influenced by the nature of the political and religious environment within which it operated. (1977, p. 99)

Finally, we might ask to what extent the four main attitudes of religious opinion identified by Tawney can be discerned in the case of social policy in Eire. It is probably true that, at different periods, all four attitudes have been displayed. Certainly there have been points at which questions of social welfare have been regarded as no concern of the Church, except to ensure that its teachings were not contravened. The Catholic Church has also, both explicitly and implicitly, accepted the existence of social inequality as necessary and desirable. The relief of poverty (through voluntary and charitable efforts) was a means by which the non-poor could attain salvation. This attitude is illustrated by one reaction to Dr Dignan's proposals for a national insurance scheme in 1944. An opponent of Dr Dignan's plan, the Bishop of Clonfert, wrote that it was un-Christian because, 'it aimed at doing away with poverty and consequently the opportunity of practising Christian charity' (quoted in Kaim-Caudle, 1967, p. 43).

The case of Eire, therefore, provides an example of the essentially conservative influence of religious ideas and beliefs on social policy. Although the Catholic Church in Eire has, since the 1960s, become rather more liberal in its attitude towards State-provided social programmes it tends to view social reform with a grudging reluctance. Its position now seems to be to acquiesce rather than to take initiatives to prevent change. In certain respects Eire represents an extreme case and one would not necessarily expect to find the pattern of religious and social development replicated in other societies. We turn now, therefore, to look at other religious influences in other contexts.

Social policy and the Protestant Ethic

Although the influence of Catholicism has been felt in countries outside Eire, such as England, America, Germany, Italy and the Netherlands, other religious ideologies have often predominated. In many countries of the West it has been Protestantism which inspired early efforts to provide welfare facilities. Although the expression of Protestant thought differed quite significantly from the tenets of Catholicism the actual effects on policy were often similar. While Protestants emphasized the virtues of individualism, as against the particular brand of collectivism advocated by Catholics, both were reluctant to accord too great a role to the State as a provider of welfare. However, although Catholics were suspicious of social provision outside the context of the family and community they had emphasized the importance of social responsibility and the need to relieve suffering. The teachings of Protestantism which, in many countries, came to supersede those of Catholicism were altogether more unrelenting and harsh. As Feagin has remarked, the institutional care for orphans, the sick and the poor which had been developed under Catholicism was

> often not continued or inaugurated by early Protestants . . . for the Protestant concern with the individual Christian and with work as a calling brought about a de-emphasis on institutionalized charity under church auspices. Emergent Protestant thought brought a new burden for Europe's poor, replacing the benevolent paternalism of Catholicism with a variable, but usually harsh morality of Protestantism. Many Protestant leaders were, at best, suspicious of the poor and were convinced that individual morality was the key issue in dealing with poverty. Maintaining the work incentive of the poor was a critical concern. (1975, p. 15)

For several centuries, until the onset of industrialism in the mid-nineteenth century, the Church was the main provider and organizer of welfare in America, Russia and Western Europe.

The parish was often the main administrative unit for the distribution of poor relief and it was usually controlled by the clergy, with the help of churchwardens, overseers and justices of the peace. The role of the Church as a provider of welfare was long-established and records show that it was a source of support during, and even before, the mediaeval period in most countries. Madison, for example, dates Church provision in Russia from 996 AD. In that year the Grand Duke Vladimir:

> issued a poor code that made the church responsible for the care and supervision of the poor, sick, aged and disabled. . . Vladimir's policy dominated Russian welfare practices until the close of the seventeenth century; attempts to relieve poverty were guided largely by the Christian precepts of charity and love and were administered directly or indirectly by the clergy. (1968, p. 3)

This pattern was repeated, with some variations in detail, in most other countries for which we have data. The scope of charitable and church interests was very wide. As Woodroofe has observed:

> Reform of prisons and lunatic asylums, the care of orphans, the provision of schools and the abolition of slavery were considered to be grist to the philanthropic mill no less than the care of the poor, the aged and the sick and different methods were evolved to meet these different needs. (1962, p. 19)

As industrialization and urbanization advanced, the Churches were increasingly unable to provide for the new needs of complex and mobile societies, and secular forms of aid began to be sought.

With the threat of increasing State intervention, in the nineteenth century, in many aspects of life Protestants, non-conformists and Catholics alike became concerned to preserve individual freedom and to encourage self-help. Many, especially in Britain and America, were influenced by the exhortations of Samuel Smiles in his book *Self Help*, where he argued that:

> 'Heaven helps those who help themselves' is a well-tried maxim, embodying in a small compass the results of vast human experience. The spirit of self-help is the root of all genuine growth in the individual; and exhibited in the lives of the many it constitutes the true source of national vigour and strength. Help from

> without is often enfeebling in its effects but help from within invariably invigorates. (1859, p. 1)

The views of Smiles coincided, in important respects, not only with those of the Christian Church but with the views of influential men like David Ricardo, Thomas Malthus and John Stuart Mill. The notions of self-help, freedom of the individual and the work ethic, although reflected in many aspects of social policy, were particularly evident in the practice and organization of social work in Britain and America. Many of the theories and methods of social work, as it was first practised, originated in the ideas of the Charity Organization Society and, in particular, those of its Secretary Charles Stewart Loch. He maintained that the indiscriminate giving of relief by Church, State and private charities was harmful to the individual because it encouraged his dependence. He, therefore, argued that relief-giving should be conducted on the basis of a set of clearly enunciated principles, designed to foster the independence of the poor and to strengthen the family. Caseworkers would be expected to investigate fully the circumstances of people seeking relief and they would need to inform themselves of the resources available to meet their needs. Woodroofe explains that, 'The type of assistance of which the Society approved was individual, personal, temporary and reformatory', and Loch firmly denounced the notion of 'the State as caterer-in-chief for its citizens' (Woodroofe, 1962, p. 39).

The principles of relief-giving were the basis of what Loch envisaged as:

> a nobler, more devoted, more scientific religious charity. . . . It could help us to realise in society the religion of charity without the sectarianism of religion. (Quoted in Woodroofe, 1962, pp. 31–2)

However, the COS was quite ruthless in its condemnation of what is regarded as indiscriminate alms-giving. In America, for example, it campaigned vigorously for the abolition of outdoor relief and was successful, in some cities, in halting the distribution of food and coal during the winter months.

It was assumed that the causes of social problems — at least amongst the vast majority of the 'undeserving' poor — lay within individuals themselves. All men, it was argued, began with the same capacities and it was up to each one to develop his talents to the full and to make a decent living for himself. If the causes of problems were 'internal' rather than external to the individual it was argued that they would best be overcome by education, rehabilitation and therapy. Money and other aid was only to be given as part of a carefully devised plan tailored to individual circumstances and would be given in such a way as to ensure that the recipient benefited from budgeting and planning its usage. According to Komisar:

> the COS believed that although public relief tended to promote dependence and pauperism, private aid given according to charity organisation rules could be used to build the character of the poor, encouraging them to be industrious and to practice thrift. (Komisar, 1974, p. 33)

The COS presented something of a paradox. As Derek Fraser has remarked it was both 'professionally pioneering but ideologically reactionary' (1973, p. 121). It established careful ground rules for the practice of social work, based on Christian ethics but, at the same time, it was:

> ferociously individualist in ideology, resisting until well into the twentieth century every important legislative measure of social welfare; from school meals to old age pensions. (Fido, 1977, p. 207)

Not all religious groups, however, supported the approach of the COS and their solutions to social problems. General Booth, of the Salvation Army, for example, argued that the roots of poverty were to be found within society itself. It was impracticable, therefore, to leave the solution to self-help and to allow those who didn't help themselves to sink. What we want, he claimed, is:

> a Social Lifeboat Institution, a Social Lifeboat Brigade, to snatch from the abyss those who, if left to themselves, will perish as miserably as the crew of the ship that founders in mid-ocean. (Quoted in Woodroofe, 1962, p. 59a)

The style of the Salvation Army was considerably more brash and interventionist than that of the COS. On the assumption that public houses and other sources of popular entertainment were the root of most social problems they went out into the streets, the music halls, the theatres and the boxing booths to practice their social work. Bailey reports that:

> On Sundays, when the urban poor were at their leisure, the Salvationists went into the streets on two or even three separate occasions, singing hymns adapted for their audience — 'Out of the Gutter we pick them up' — led by officers in red guernseys ornamented with religious texts. (1977, p. 237)

Such attempted conversions often resulted in rioting and the erection of barriers in working-class streets to repel the invaders.

Although differing in their approach many religious groups in Britain in the nineteenth and early twentieth century opposed the extension of State involvement in social welfare. They argued that certain inequalities were justified and that, where help was needed, it should be provided, selectively, by religious and other voluntary organizations. Considerable attention was focused on the importance of preserving the freedom of the individual and encouraging his independence. These attitudes were also expressed, if anything, with even greater conviction in America than in the countries of Western Europe. Although America has often been described as a 'melting pot' in which different races and religious creeds are eventually united we can see that it has been the views of White Anglo-Saxon Protestant (WASPs) which have been most influential on social policy. As Dorothy James remarks, 'Calvinist thought shaped the values of most of the early settlers of America, including English Pilgrims and Puritans, French Huguenots, Scots, and the Dutch' (1972, p. 28).

Protestantism (especially Calvinism) provided a strong rationale for materialistic individualism and for the growth of capitalism. It found one of its purest forms in the work of W.G. Sumner who argued that God had ordained the social order and that the truly talented would come to dominance through the 'survival of the fittest'. As James observes:

> The harsh implications of Sumner's theory for the poor are obvious. And most Protestant churches did not soften them by a counter emphasis on charity. Social Darwinism was the justification for the business community's actions which business accepted; and the Protestant churches supported business, providing religious sanction for the businessman's views with respect to poverty, inequality, stewardship, state aid and labor. Taking a

> negative view of social reform and state action, they stressed individual regeneration. (1972, p. 30)

As we shall see in the next two chapters the Protestant Ethic has remained a powerful influence on contemporary social policy in America, emphasizing both the need to enhance the work incentive and the appropriateness of private and voluntary efforts as against State aid.

Generally speaking, therefore, we can conclude that the impact of Protestantism on social policy historically has been to retard social reform. In combination with its natural allies 'liberalism' and '*laissez-faire*' it challenged the role of the State as a provider of welfare and emphasized the desirability of self-help. In many countries, however, the trenchant views adopted by nineteenth-century Protestants have been softened and the Church and clergy are no longer so opposed to the existence of State-provided social services; indeed they may co-operate fully with their local representatives. At the same time in other countries, such as America, Protestantism, in its various manifestations, has had a stronger hold and its influence is still reactionary and pervasive. The basic principles of Protestantism are expressed both in religious and 'secularized' forms and are frequently used as a rationale for non-intervention by the State.

The secularization of social policy

One of the most important stages in the development of social policy in any country is the point at which social welfare functions become 'secularized'. Unfortunately, information on this complex transitional phase is extremely limited so that the points made in this discussion are necessarily speculative. More informed analysis must await further detailed research. In most countries of Western Europe the secularization of social policy occurred during a period (usually the sixteenth or seventeenth century) on which documentary evidence is incomplete so that we can sketch in only the broadest outline of how change was accomplished. It is all the more important, therefore, to examine developments in countries such as Eire, in which the process might still be said to be evolving. Despite the limitations of our knowledge of the process of secularization in social policy, we can begin to piece together a number of general propositions.

Essentially we need to ask the following questions: What form does secularization actually take — does the State simply take over the functions once performed by the Church (poor relief, education, care of the sick and elderly, etc.)? What kind of time-span is involved — does secularization of all functions occur at the same time, or is it staggered? Is secularization a 'once-and-for-all' process or do certain tasks eventually revert to the Church? Does secularization always coincide with the onset of industrialization and urbanization or might other developments initiate the process? Why does secularization occur at different periods in different societies and, indeed, why does it occur at all? With our present state of knowledge we can only begin to answer some of these questions satisfactorily but, nevertheless, some trends do present themselves.

We can discern at least two interpretations of the secularization of social policy, in the literature. The first contends that as societies become more complex, as a result of industrialization and urbanization, and as mobility of the workforce increases, it no longer becomes appropriate to rely on a highly localized system of social welfare based on the Church.

It is argued that the Church has neither the resources nor the organization to provide support on the scale and complexity which becomes necessary as a result of societal change. Larger units of government must take over the responsibilities of raising revenue, of determining eligibility and of dispensing aid. The second holds that as religion ceases to exert social controls (and to be the 'opiate of the masses'), other forms of control which will secure the conformity of the working classes must be introduced. Where once religious teaching legitimized inequality within society secular social policies now aim, if not to justify social divisions, at least to mitigate their worst excesses.

Heclo's account of the development of social policy in Britain and Sweden is one of the few attempts to illustrate the changes which took place during the period of secularization and to assess their importance. In doing so he tends to combine the two interpretations of change outlined above.

The 'vital change' occurred, he argues, with the supplantation of the Catholic Church in Britain and Sweden and the establishment of 'state churches'. At this point:

> the state for the first time assumed ultimate responsibility for the care of the poor. Any immediate changes in the treatment of the poor were probably small and parishes as local administrative

> units survived for 400 years in each country. But in principle, and in the long term, the change from religious duty to state authority was crucial. State responsibility meant a fundamental alteration in the previous religious perspective, despite the politics and corrupt dispensations which had crept into religion's appeal to charitable values. If the Church was concerned primarily with virtues of the giver, the state was concerned with maintaining social order. (Heclo, 1974, p. 48)

This important change took place, Heclo argues, partly as a means of controlling beggars and vagrants and partly because the Church was no longer able to cope with the problem of the poor. One of the main motivations for the establishment of a State system of poor relief, he claims, was to counteract the effects of indiscriminate alms-giving by the Church (a view expressed by other writers). It was argued that the Church had actually pauperized a large class of dependent poor and that new and stricter regulations were needed for the distribution of relief. Interestingly, Heclo suggests that such developments were not simply the result of particular internal forces within Britain and Sweden, but that they were part of a European movement of reform.

> The most important point here is to recognise the essentially international character of these attempts at developing secular alternatives in social policy. The period 1490–1530 saw a vast upsurge of such reformist zeal in the European market for social policy ideas. Poor relief reform became a major topic of leading thinkers across the continent. (Heclo, 1974, p. 49)

These observations illustrate the importance of one of the determinants of social policy discussed in the last chapter — the cultural diffusion factor (identified by Vladimir Rys). It is clear that cultural diffusion, then, did not wait upon the introduction of mass travel or the media, or colonialism, or upon the development of internationally based social research. Policy ideas were obviously being exchanged and discussed on a supranational basis as early as the fifteenth century. Heclo warns, however, that:

> One should not . . . confuse the essentially international scope of policy deliberations with effective policy as implemented. Rarely has the gap between promise and performance been greater. (1974, p. 50)

Although the discussion, and to some extent the formulation of policy, took place at the international level the administration of systems of poor relief in Europe was still highly localized and became the responsibility of justices of the peace, overseers of the poor and churchwardens.

Rimlinger's interpretation of the secularization of social policy in Europe is essentially similar:

> In England, France and other European countries, governments became concerned with the lot of the poor not for purposes of relieving suffering, but for the maintenance of law and order. The legislation relating to the poor began with measures to punish beggars and kept its repressive character until recent times. . . . Private charity was inadequate to cope with the size of the problem. Moreover, it was recognized that indiscriminate charity often contributed to the problem of pauperism. Mediaeval charity had a tendency toward being indiscriminate, since its major motivation was the salvation of the giver rather than the behaviour of the recipient. (1971, p. 19)

Joe Feagin, using as his source the Webb's *English Poor Law History Vol. 1* also supports this view:

> The concern of the ruling elites was not so much with Christian duty as with maintaining order. Government control of the mobile, able-bodied worker, as well as the criminal, was deemed to be more important than government relief to the poor, but both were to a substantial degree a manifestation of social control. (Feagin, 1975, p. 19)

These three accounts seem to concur on a number of important points — although, since they are all based on the same secondary sources (the Webbs), this may not be surprising and may, indeed, bias their conclusions. All, however, date the first period of secularization in social policy from the time of the Reformation. Each suggests that secularization resulted both from the inability of the Church to deal with changing economic circumstances and the necessity of controlling increasing numbers of beggars and vagrants. We can see that within a relatively short space of time, the State replaced a relatively simple system of poor relief with an equally simple (though more repressive) system.

However, as Tawney has argued (and as Heclo implies) the

transference of responsibility from Church to State was not a neat and clear-cut transition:

> After, as before, the Reformation the parish continued to be a community in which religious and social obligations were inextricably intertwined, and it was as a parishioner, rather than as a subject of the secular authority, that he bore his share of public burdens and performed such public functions as fell to his lot. (Tawney, 1966, p. 159)

It was still the Church which owned property and received bequests and which provided any education that might be available. The Church was also recognized as being the main source of 'official' information so it was hardly surprising that:

> It was to the clergy and the parochial organization that the State turned in coping with pauperism, and down to 1597 collectors for the poor were chosen by the churchwardens in conjunction with the parson. (Tawney, 1966, p. 159)

By this stage there was no real specialization of functions — with respect to health, housing, education, etc. — as occurred later in industrializing societies. Further stages of secularization can be identified — usually in the nineteenth century — in these different policy areas. Despite the fact that the responsibility for basic poor relief was taken from the Church in most (not all) European countries after the Reformation, the clergy were not prohibited from establishing other services. They set up alms-houses, hospitals, orphanages, schools and other institutions, and we can see that disparate attempts at secularization in all these different spheres occurred with varying degrees of success.

Very often it was the field of educational policy which was the main battleground for disputes about control between the Church and the State. Whyte, for example, charts the varying fortunes of the Catholic Church in its attempt to develop or retain denominational education:

> In some countries, such as Soviet Russia, the Church has been forbidden to operate schools altogether. In others such as the United States, Australia, or France under the Third Republic, it has been free to operate schools but has received no direct support from public funds. In others again, such as England and

> Northern Ireland, Catholic schools receive substantial aid from the State but not quite so much as the schools directly maintained by local authorities. (Whyte, 1971, p. 16)

Furthermore, the secularization of education was not a single problem. In pluralistic societies education was fragmented denominationally and provided by a variety of religious groupings. Each of their cases for the retention of control of the schools, and in some cases the universities, had to be judged on its own merits. In Britain, at least, Fraser has argued that the rationale for secularization was expressed not so much in terms of the particular virtues of State control *per se* but as a response to the inadequacies of voluntarism and the existing system of education:

> It was wholly typical of the way social policy developed in the second quarter of the nineteenth century that Parliament's concern for education should originate not from some overall general conviction about the role of state education but as a pragmatic response to these deficiencies. (Fraser, 1973, p. 74)

Secularization was not achieved at a specific point in time by an Act of Parliament but it was a gradual process of compromise and the relaxation of controls. As in other contexts (for example, the United States) the offer of resources for education by the State was followed by increasing control over how those resources were administered. The religious case was strongly fought, however, and secularization was only achieved amidst considerable conflict and controversy. In Eire (which provides a contrast on most of these points) secularization of education is far from being complete, although the hold of the Church over the schools is steadily weakening and the clergy make up a decreasing proportion of the teaching staff. In other areas of social policy Eire gives the appearance of having acquiesced to secularization. There are quite well-established public income maintenance schemes, family allowances, housing programmes, a limited system of free medical care and other miscellaneous benefits such as free travel, free footwear and free electricity. Moreover, the percentage of GNP devoted to social security, health and welfare programmes has risen, quite significantly, from 13.2 per cent in 1970 to 20.4 per cent in 1975 (Social indicators for the European Community 1960–1975, EEC Brussels, 1977). Even so the clergy still exert an important influence and it would be wrong to conclude that the process of secularization is complete. As Basil Chubb remarks, 'The Catholic Church is in a unique position as an interest group. It is the only great corporate institution in the community that rivals, indeed, towers over those of the political system' (1963). The power of the Catholic Church has meant that, as far as social policy is concerned, Eire has lagged behind most other European countries in the extent of secularization which has been achieved.

The real question, however, is whether these trends which we have described above can form part of a general explanation about the process of secularization in social policy or whether they are peculiar to their European context. Unfortunately, the information which we would need in order to answer this question fully is not readily available, but we can make some preliminary comparisons. America presents an interesting case; the first phase of secularization in European social policy had virtually been completed when the first European settlers went to America. They took with them, then, an already secularized system. In some areas the Church and the parish remained the primary administrative units but there were others, notably in New England, in which the town meeting made the policy decisions and administered relief. Religious fragmentation and hostility to government resulted, as we have argued earlier, in the subsequent development of an extensive network of Church-based, denominational social services. Superficially, at least, the pattern of secularization which evolved in Europe therefore seems to have been reversed in America, in certain respects. Beginning with a framework of already secularized services, America moved on to develop voluntary programmes, reverting again to secularized public services in the 1930s.

If we look elsewhere to test out our general hypothesis we can see that other countries fit the European model more closely. Bernice Madison, in a brief analysis of secularization in Russian social policy, concludes, for example, that:

> In progressing slowly from church inspired charity to public responsibility for welfare, and in permitting privately supported charity as an expression of community concern Russia resembled other European countries — but was far behind them. Catherine's prikazy created in 1775, typified the ambivalence with which the government accepted responsibility for welfare institutions — a responsibility clearly enunciated in England, for example, by the Act of 1536. (1968, p. 22)

The process of secularization in Russian social policy essentially began with Peter the Great (1682–1725). He established that it should be municipal government, rather than the Church, which would have ultimate responsibility for the poor. The giving of alms was forbidden and any private donations were to be made to the government and to State-run institutions. The regime was repressive and control of welfare institutions often fell to the police. Catherine the Great (1762–96) developed the principle of public responsibility yet further, although in a more humane manner. Each province was to have a Committee on Public Assistance (prikaz) which was to establish and maintain public institutions and to regulate the activities of private charities. The result was that, 'the duty of caring for the poor was more firmly placed on local authorities, and a diversified network of specialized agencies was established' (Madison, 1968, p. 9). Again we can attribute the causes of secularization partly to a reaction against the inefficiency of private charity and partly to a desire for new methods of controlling begging and the 'undeserving' poor.

These examples from different societies do indicate, therefore, that there are a number of common trends in the pattern which the secularization of social policy tends to follow. The secularization of rudimentary Church-based poor relief often occurs at a stage when the economy is becoming more complex and freer markets and wage labour become prevalent. There is frequently a dissatisfaction both with the inconsistencies of voluntary support and with the effects of indiscriminate alms-giving. Secularization of responsibility, therefore, is seen as a means of plugging the gaps in provision for the 'deserving' but also of ensuring stricter conditions and a harsher regime for the 'undeserving'. After this first stage of secularization we may also observe secondary stages of secularization in different areas of policy as they become more specialized. Even when major functions have been secularized the Church often retains a role in the voluntary sector and provides services which the State cannot or will not offer. Secularization is rarely accomplished with great speed and there is often a lengthy transitional period in which the Church provides the administrative structure for State services. However, it would be premature to suggest that these few observations constitute a 'theory' of secularization in social policy and, as we have indicated, there are a number of important exceptions which tend to call into question any general explanations which we may produce.

Conclusion

The purpose of this chapter has been to show that religious ideas can, in some contexts, be an important determinant of social policy. We have also indicated that the development of an historical perspective is an important part of comparative analysis and that useful data can be collected both for different societies and for one society at different periods of time. It would be wrong to conclude that conservative religious forces are always lurking in the background ready to stamp out social reform in any country in which it rears its head. In most industrialized and urbanized countries the Church is only one interest group among many and has few visible effects on the way in which social policy evolves. In other societies, however, which are still predominantly agricultural and rural and where a single religious group has almost complete control (such as Eire) the effects are clearly more striking. At the same time, in industrialized countries where the role of the State in social welfare is relatively limited and where religious affiliation and participation is high (as in America) — even though there are many competing religious groups — the influence of religious ideas may also be quite marked. In many cases, too, the intertwined strands of racial and religious affiliation may also be important, for example, in the attempt to develop national systems of education for children of different racial, religious, cultural and linguistic backgrounds. The simple message for the intending student, therefore, is to be aware that religion can be and has been an important determinant of social policy but one should not necessarily expect to find powerful religious influences in every society which is being examined.

CHAPTER 6

Work and Welfare

One of the most important questions which all societies with systems of social policy have faced is how to provide support for the needy without, at the same time, undermining their incentive to work. The problem arises of how to ensure that levels of benefit are sufficiently high for the maintenance of a tolerable standard of living but not too high to discourage the poor from seeking work. Although most industrial societies have accepted at least some degree of responsibility for the 'impotent poor' — the sick and disabled, the elderly and children — the question of how to deal with the 'able-bodied' poor has always been a matter of controversy. An analysis of ways in which different societies, at different periods, have solved this fundamental dilemma, of the proper relationship between work and welfare, is often revealing. There are a number of dimensions to this relationship and we shall explore some of them in the sections which follow. We begin by looking at the ways in which ideas about work, attitudes to work and the 'work ethic' have influenced social policy, cross-nationally, over many centuries.

Welfare and the work ethic: the historical perspective

Some of the earliest discussions about work and welfare arose in debates about the Poor Laws in Europe and America. As we have suggested in the last chapter, a series of social and economic changes in European countries which resulted, in most of them, in some degree of secularization gave rise to new outlooks in social welfare. Mencher argues that the establishment of poor laws in the sixteenth century marked the beginning of 'the modern era of welfare policy'. Since then:

> the focal issue for all economic security policy . . . has been the treatment of the able-bodied or potentially productive indivi-

> dual. . . . For example, to what extent should the employable group be held responsible for impotent individuals dependent on them? To what extent should all individuals be expected to provide from their previous earnings for their incapacity or lack of employment? The treatment of the able-bodied or employable has thus been the most continuous and controversial concern of economic security policy. (Mencher, 1967, pp. xvi–xvii)

The concern about how to deal with the employable poor was almost universal, in Europe, during this period and is discussed by a number of writers (see Rimlinger, 1971; Heclo, 1974). It achieved prominence for several reasons but two were of particular importance. Firstly, there were the moral and religious views about the inherent value of work and the virtue of hard work as a means of character building but, secondly, there was fear of the violence and social disruption which might result from the deprivation and frustration of the employable but unemployed. There was also the practical question of how to deal with vagrancy and medicancy and whose responsibility vagrants would be.

The relationship between welfare and the work ethic under the English Poor Law has been quite extensively documented but we can see that similar dilemmas arose and similar debates were conducted in many countries during the same period. Heclo, for example, has shown that the development of poor relief policy in Sweden passed through similar stages to that in England, although there were certain significant differences in local practice. Each began with Church-based charity, moved into a phase of State control, and then to the establishment of poor laws which he describes as 'deliberate . . . attempts at social engineering' (1974, p. 47). The administration of Swedish poor law policy was, on the whole, more centralized, there were fewer workhouses and a greater tolerance of mendicancy. There was also much less reliance on the supplementation of low wages from public funds which became widespread in England after 1795 (and was known as the Speenhamland system). However, the Swedish system (like the English) was faced with the problems of how to deal with the unemployed vagrant (and whether to regard him/her as criminal) and how to contain the costs of an increasingly expensive public relief system. The outcome, as Heclo points out, was that, 'As in Britain, Swedish policy fluctuated between concerns for adequacy and economic restrictiveness' (1974, p. 62).

By the end of the nineteenth century both Britain and Sweden had made firm attempts to abolish outdoor relief to the able-bodied as a means of cutting costs. However, local practices differed and in some areas of Britain minimum support was still offered to those prepared to work for it. In Sweden the central government required localities to provide work for the able-bodied but again practices varied and some localities did so while others did not. The outcome was that:

> at the end of the nineteenth century the poor law in Britain and Sweden was being increasingly strained by that troublesome category of the poor who were neither infirm nor working. In both countries, poor relief, with its accompanying disgrace and opprobrium, remained the only major avenue open to the unemployed citizen seeking state aid. (Heclo, 1974, p. 65)

Similar developments occurred elsewhere. In France, for example the same distinction was maintained between the impotent (or 'deserving') poor and the able-bodied (or 'undeserving') poor. As Rimlinger remarks, the French decrees relating to the poor resembled the British in that, 'they combined provisions for the relief of invalids with threats of repression and the obligation to work for able-bodied paupers' (1971, p. 24). A variety of public works programmes was established, often with the assistance of the clergy. Later, as harsher regimes evolved, some of the able-bodied were set to work digging canals or in galleys while others were simply locked up. Notions of both the 'right' and the 'duty' to work became clearly enunciated during the period of the Revolution. The view became quite widely held that:

> the duty of society is . . . to seek to prevent misfortune, to relieve it, to offer work to those who need it in order to live, to force them if they refuse to work, and finally to assist without work those whose age or infirmity deprive them of the ability to work. (Quoted in Rimlinger, 1971, p. 30)

Rimlinger also indicates that, during the same years, similar kinds of belief were evident in Germany. The Prussian Landrecht (Civil Code) which came into force in 1794, for example, established that:

> Work adapted to their strength and capacities shall be supplied to those who lack means and opportunity of earning a livelihood

> for themselves and for those dependent upon them. (Quoted in Rimlinger, 1971, p. 94)

For those who refused the opportunities to work which were offered them the State, it was argued, had the right to compel, or to punish them.

America, too, inherited many of the same problems of the European Poor Laws — how, and on what basis, to give relief to the able-bodied and how to encourage the habit of work. Most of the colonies introduced systems of both 'outdoor' and 'indoor' relief by which the needy could be assisted either in their own homes, with food, clothing or small allowances, or in institutions such as almshouses and orphanages. Later, as in England, there were moves to abolish outdoor relief on the grounds that it encouraged dependency and idleness and, by the end of the nineteenth century, the only help available to many of the poor was 'indoor relief' in workhouses and poor farms. The increasingly harsh restrictions of the nineteenth century were prompted by the fear that if the pauper were given relief too readily he/she would become a permanent drain on resources and would cease to seek gainful employment. Indoor relief, therefore, was thought to be preferable:

> The proponents of the almshouses argued that they saved money because they deterred people from becoming paupers, they got work out of those who entered them so that recipients helped pay the cost of their keep, and they instilled work habits in those who must have been idle. (Komisar, 1974, p. 29)

Although there were some variations in how the poor laws were administered both *within* European countries and America and *between* them, a number of common themes emerged up to and during the nineteenth century. One of these was that distinction which was made, both in principle and in practice, between the impotent and the 'able-bodied' poor. As Mencher has observed, there was general acceptance of the need to provide for those — such as the sick or the elderly — who had become dependent through no fault of their own. The real problem was how to deal with the group who were able to work to support themselves and their families but who, for various reasons, were not doing so.

The concern about the able-bodied poor also coincided, in most countries, with the shift away from local, charitable forms of care and towards national systems of public support. The problem came to be recognized as one of almost universal significance which many areas shared and not one which was peculiar to individual localities. As Rimlinger put it:

> poverty, in effect, became a matter of national concern almost from the beginning of the modern nation-state. Not surprisingly, the question of how to treat the labouring poor occupied an important place in the minds of those who concerned themselves with national economic policy. (1971, p. 13)

Related to this shift in emphasis was another which indicated that the problems were not simply those of individual poor people but that they raised questions about relations in the wider society. Mencher, for example, shows that:

> The focus of economic security became the relationship between social provision and employment. 'The question', as Alfred Marshall later stated, 'was, in fact, one of unemployment rather than poor relief [and] to both seventeenth and eighteenth century writers the crux of the problem was the position of the able Poor'. (1967, p. 50)

A further matter of principle was raised, concerning the treatment of the able-bodied. This was whether they should be regarded as criminal, and therefore punished, or whether they should be regarded as unfortunate, and rehabilitated. The way in which the problem was defined, of course, led to different views about how it should be solved. This dilemma was never fully resolved. Poor relief policies in different countries, from the fifteenth century onwards, reflect shifting attitudes towards the causes of unemployment. At certain periods 'individualistic' explanations prevail — the cause of the problem is said to be an unwillingness or inability on the part of the individual to seek and engage in work. At other periods, 'structuralist' explanations have been advanced to show that the problems of the able-bodied poor have their roots in the structure of the labour market, in the unavailability of jobs in the right place at the right time and in low wage work. Where the pauper was held to be culpable he/she was punished by forced labour or by incarceration in an institution or, latterly, by more subtle administrative techniques of exclusion. Where he/she was thought capable of benefiting from rehabilitation he/she was offered counselling, moral guidance, training and work experience programmes.

The central importance of work and the worker became established as a matter of concern for social policy, therefore, at a very early stage in the development of public systems of welfare in Europe and America. As these countries moved into the twentieth century the issues facing them remained somewhat similar, although their responses to them often differed. It is interesting that, in most countries, the first national social security programme to be enacted was usually some form of compensation for injury at work. Germany developed such a programme in 1884 and was followed by Britain in 1897, Denmark, France and Italy (1898), Sweden and the Netherlands (1901) and the United States (1908) (see Heidenheimer et al., 1976, p. 189). Unemployment insurance was originally confined to specific groups of the labour force before eventually being extended to provide universal coverage. Although provision for the unemployed, generally, may have lagged behind that for other groups, the issue of unemployment was still a matter of great debate. Heclo suggests, for example, that:

> Unemployment was not the first area of need to be attacked by modern social policy, but it was perhaps the most strategic. For four centuries the driving concern behind most changes in poor law policy had been the problem of the 'able-bodied poor'. Undoubtedly a key reason for this policy attention to the able-bodied over all other needy groups lay in the state's concern with poor relief as a tool of social order; it was not the sick or infirm who burned hayricks and broke shop windows. (1974, p. 65)

This leads us to a further issue in the relationship between work and welfare, which is the hypothesis that the main aim of social policy is not to help the needy or to relieve suffering but it is to pacify the unemployed, on the one hand, and to enforce low-wage work on the other.

However, before going on to examine this idea in detail one other point needs to be made. It would be wrong to give the impression that strengthening the work ethic has only been an important feature of social policy in Western capitalist societies or in countries in which the 'Protestant Ethic' has been a formative influence. A brief examination of other societies shows that the use of social policy to maintain incentives to work is a far more widespread phenomenon. Titmuss suggests, for example, that:

> Soviet Russia . . . has fashioned a model of social welfare which

> is based, in large measure, on the principles of work-performance, achievement and meritocratic selection. Wage and salary differentials between the top and bottom of the Russian Civil Service . . . are larger than wage-salary differentials in the British Civil Service. The social security system tends to legitimate — even enhance — these differentials. . . . Other Soviet social services — like the mental health service — are, in part, social control mechanisms (they perform a police function) in respect of dissenters, non-conformers, deviants and underachievers. In part, they also function to sustain and glorify the work ethic (as do the boarding schools in Russia which are preoccupied with character-building and the value of hard physical labour). (1974, p. 17)

Madison's more detailed account of the relationship between work and welfare in Russia also supports this view. She suggests:

> One of the central ideas in Soviet helping methods is that work . . . aids in the regeneration process, improves the moral and physical condition of the invalid and satisfies his natural urge to participate in his country's development. (1968, p. 186)

The origin of this belief is said to be the Pavlovian dictum that work gives personal satisfaction and that every individual should be enabled to take part in work activities.

From a rather different context Abraham Doron makes a very similar point. In Israeli society, too, he argues, there has been considerable emphasis on providing welfare in a way which will promote incentives to work. At the same time, there appears to be less commitment, than has traditionally been the case in Europe, to assisting the 'impotent' poor and those incapable of work.

> In line with the major values of Israeli society, which have their origin in Zionist ideology, the chief concern of society should be to assure productive work for all. The 'work ethic' and, often, even the 'religion of labour' still occupy a central place in the value system of Israeli society. The concern for the needy who do not work is therefore of low priority. Assistance provisions are regarded as a transitionary necessity until all needy people have been individually rehabilitated and until the Israeli society and economy as a collectivity are able to absorb them in productive work. (Doron, 1978, p. 442)

These brief examples, therefore, suggest that the relationship between work and welfare has been a central focus — often a problematic one — of social policy in different societies, both historically and cross-nationally. One question we need to answer is why a broadly similar problem has been dealt with in different ways in different situations. Why have some societies developed policies which have sought, essentially, to rehabilitate the able-bodied poor and return them to the labour market while others have sought to punish them for infringing a basic societal obligation — the duty to work? We can identify a moral rationale underpinning the work ethic as well as religious, economic and political reasons. The next section looks more closely at some of these issues.

Work, welfare and social control

One of the most detailed attempts to examine the work incentive aspects of social policy from a comparative perspective, is that made by Piven and Cloward (1972). Their view, forcefully expressed, is that social policy is concerned not with the relief of suffering or the reduction of inequalities but with two distinct purposes, one of which is to maintain social order while the other is to enforce low-wage work. Social policy, then, is seen as but one aspect of economic policy and it is governed primarily by economic requirements rather than by social need. Thus, Piven and Cloward argue:

> Relief arrangements are ancillary to economic arrangements. Their chief function is to regulate labour, and they do that in two general ways. First, when mass unemployment leads to outbreaks of turmoil, relief programs are ordinarily initiated or expanded to absorb and control enough of the unemployed to restore order; then as turbulence subsides, the relief system contracts, expelling those who are needed to populate the labour market. Relief also performs a labor-regulating function in this shrunken state, however. Some of the aged, the disabled, the insane and others who are no use as workers are left on the relief rolls, and their treatment is so degrading and punitive as to instill in the labouring masses a fear of the fate that awaits them should they relax into beggary and pauperism. To demean and punish those who do not work is to exalt by contrast even the meanest labor at the meanest wages. (1972, pp. 3–4)

In support of this view Piven and Cloward draw on wide-ranging evidence from Europe in the sixteenth century to contemporary America. Their argument, essentially, is that the stability of society is maintained primarily by the conditioning of the mass of the population into specific work roles. When this pattern is disrupted by unemployment, by migration or by other factors, such as bad harvests, other forms of control (they argue) are needed to prevent disruption and civil disorder. Ideally these new forms of control should be directed towards supporting the work role and should wither away once the immediate crisis is past.

> Because the market is unable to control men's behaviour, at least for a time, a surrogate system of social control must be evolved, at least for a time. Moreover, if the surrogate system is to be consistent with normally dominant patterns, it must restore people to work roles. (pp. 7–8)

In such a view the relationship between the provision of welfare, attitudes to work and labour market policies is very marked and these concerns are inextricably bound up together. Piven and Cloward, then, set out to show that welfare policies functioned in a coercive manner under poor laws in France, England, Germany, Ireland and other European countries. With the coming of more liberal and more comprehensive social policies during the early twentieth century throughout Europe (and to a more limited extent in America) the issues, however, remained alive, and when the Stock Market crashed in 1929 in America, and mass unemployment ensued, the traditional relationships between work and welfare rapidly became re-established. By 1933, when 15 million workers were unemployed, the Federal Government belatedly took action to relieve distress. Out of a series of relief measures three, in particular, were directed towards the unemployed. These were the Civilian Conservation Corps, the Public Works Administration and the Federal Emergency Relief Act. The last of these, which was designed to provide direct relief 'to all needy unemployed persons and/or their dependents', quickly became unpopular, and every effort was made to transfer resources from direct relief to public works programmes. A little over a year after the Federal Emergency Relief Act had come into force, Roosevelt announced that direct relief would be abolished and that the unemployed would now be dealt with by the newly established Works Progress Administration. 'The Federal Government', he declared, 'must and shall quit this business of direct relief' (quoted in Piven and Cloward, p. 94). Financial aid to the able-bodied was quickly abandoned, therefore, once the immediate threat of disorder appeared to have abated. It was replaced by work relief which, too, became unpopular and proved to be short-lived. However, while it lasted, it served an important purpose. As Piven and Cloward put it 'By once more enmeshing people in the work role, the cornerstone of social control in any society, it went far toward moderating civil disorder' (p. 97). For the 'unemployable', a series of measures were introduced under the 1935 Social Security Act and, even here, work requirements and work incentives were gradually built into the different programmes. It was in one of these programmes — Aid to Dependent Children (later renamed as Aid to Families with Dependent Children) — that the most blatant attempts to set the poor to work, and to enforce low-wage work, took place.

AFDC quickly became the subject of controversy, in part because the expected 'withering away' of welfare, which had been anticipated when the Depression had passed, had not occurred. On the contrary, the welfare rolls were growing steadily (and in the 1960s grew dramatically) and what had been envisaged as a short-term measure for white widows and their children was becoming a source of long-term aid for black unsupported mothers and their families. During the Eisenhower administration a number of crude administrative tactics were used to remove people from the rolls. 'Suitable home', 'man-in-the-house' and 'liable relatives' clauses were invoked to deny financial assistance on the grounds that the homes in which children were being cared for were unsuitable, that women were cohabiting or that their relatives, rather than the State, should have primary responsibility for their care. One of the most widespread tactics for cutting back on ADC payments, and the most important for present purposes, was the 'employable mother' rule implemented in many States after Louisiana first introduced it in 1943. Increasing numbers of children, and women who were deemed to be 'employable', were removed from the relief rolls. In areas in which seasonal employment was available ADC payments were simply withheld as a matter of course — even if mothers were actually unable to find employment. This and similar practices ensured the availability of a large pool of mostly unskilled women who could be offered (and forced to take) low-wage work.

Such attitudes towards the employment of unsupported mothers persisted, and indeed were strengthened, in America through the 1960s and 1970s. Many of the War on Poverty programmes, instituted under the 1964 Economic Opportunity Act, reasserted the principle of the desirability of work relief (albeit in a more sophisticated form) over direct relief. The main aim of the Act was to offer new opportunities through education, work training and work experience programmes and approximately half of the War on Poverty funds in 1965 were directed towards this end. There were several measures — the Manpower Development and Training Act (1962), the Concentrated Employment Program (1967), the Emergency Employment Act (1971) and the Comprehensive Employment and Training Act (1973) — which, in their various ways, aimed to set the poor to work. Perhaps the most important policy development, however, and one in which the relationship between work, welfare and control could be seen most clearly, was the 1967 Social Security amendments with specified that women in receipt of AFDC must register for work. As Bruno Stein observed:

> The 1967 amendments marked a considerable shift in attitude toward the employability of mothers who were heads of household. The founders of the Social Security Act had viewed the mother as a homebody (and an unwelcome competitor in the labour market). . . . However, the rising labour force participation rate of women, including women with children of school age, made the working mother a commonplace spectacle on the American scene. . . . As a result, the idea that a mother's socially proper place was at home, rearing children, became increasingly foreign. (1976, pp. 20–1)

As part of the 1967 amendments a new programme — the Work Incentive Program (WIN) — was introduced with the intention of returning all the employable poor to the labour market. WIN was followed by a second programme, entitled Incentives for Independence (or the 'brownie point program') which reduced the benefits of selected individuals and allowed them to earn them back on a points scheme which gave credit for certain 'socially acceptable' activities such as the establishment of the paternity of illegitimate children and 'activities which are designed to achieve permanent and adequately compensated employment'. The Family Assistance Plan proposed by Richard Nixon, and Jimmy Carter's Better Jobs and Income Plan (neither of which reached the statute books) also marked a shift in direction from 'welfare to workfare' and would have required welfare recipients to enroll in work experience programmes.

There are many examples from American social policy for the 'employable' therefore, to illustrate the linkages between welfare policy, labour market policies and control. There is ample evidence, from the programmes discussed above, to suggest that social policies for this particular group have been determined far more by the desire to reduce welfare costs, by the backlash against welfare recipients and by the demand for low-paid workers than by any considerations of the needs of the 'employable' or the relief of poverty. Many of the measures taken to reduce the welfare rolls were also attempts to control beneficiaries by the imposition of moral standards with respect to their personal behaviour and by the eradication of the sin of idleness. In fact, many of the assumptions about the employability of mothers on welfare and their attitudes to work have proved to be ill-founded. It was estimated, when the WIN programme began, that one million AFDC families (or nearly half) could be removed from the welfare rolls between 1969–74. In the event, the great majority of AFDC recipients (around 76 per cent), even by the Department of Health Education and Welfare's own standards, were found to be unemployable by virtue of their ill health, disability, old age, lack of child care facilities and lack of education. By 1973 only 16 per cent of these mothers had actually been set to work. At the same time a series of studies (Liebow, 1967; Podell, 1969; Goodwin, 1972; Rossi and Lyall, 1976) have shown that many assumptions about the negative attitudes to work of welfare recipients are questionable and that many are keen to find work and to earn a living. The evidence suggests that it is the lack of jobs rather than the lack of incentives which keeps the poor from working.

There are several indications, therefore, that the interrelationships between work and welfare, at least in the American system, are much as Piven and Cloward describe them. There is some question about the extent to which their arguments can be applied to all social policies, including those for the unemployable (see Higgins, 1978a) but generally speaking, their hypothesis is well supported by evidence. Furthermore, we can see that their analysis has a more general validity and is not only applicable to the American situation. Many of the social reforms introduced by Bismarck in Germany in the 1880s, for example, were quite explicitly designed to control the working man by making him dependent on the State and fostering his allegiance. Thus, the nature of control was somewhat different from that envisaged by Piven and Cloward and illustrates the variations on the theme which runs through their work.

> Many of Bismarck's critics accused him, not without justification, of seeking through his legislation to make German workers 'depend' upon the state. . . . 'Welfare' soothed the spirit, or perhaps tamed it. Bismarck's deliberate invocation of 'subservience' is at the opposite end of the scale from the socialist invocation of 'equality' as the goal of the 'welfare state'. . . . The invocation was, of course, bound up with conscious political calculation. Bismarck was anxious to make German social democracy less attractive to working-men. He feared 'class war' and wanted to postpone it as long as possible. (Briggs, 1961, p. 249)

The rationale for these policies which emerged, not from an 'awakening social conscience' but from a firm basis of authoritarian State power, was the social integration of an industrializing nation. As Rimlinger remarks, social insurance represented:

> a conscious attempt at cementing the social fabric of the industrial order, with the interests of the state, instead of the welfare of the worker as the prime objective. (1971, p. 93)

Despite fundamental political shifts since social insurance was first introduced Heidenheimer et al. argue, the main features of the Germany social security system have remained much the same. They have been 'closely tied to the question of economic production' and have been concerned 'not so much with self-help or social adequacy as with protecting the capacities and incentives for gainful employment' (Heidenheimer et al., 1976, p. 200).

Russia, too, offers further examples of the close relationship between social and economic policies and the treatment of the working man. The point that social policies can be used to achieve social stability, political power and economic productivity is amply borne out and the notion that the primary function of welfare is the relief of distress called into question. The idea that benefits will necessarily be determined by some measurement of social need is also in doubt. According to Rimlinger, at least, social policy in the aftermath of the 1917 Revolution was used, crudely and explicitly, as a means of control:

> Before very long . . . social security programs became a weapon in the hands of the ruling party to strengthen its control over the working population. Benefits, eligibility conditions and administrative procedures were tailored to suit the objectives of those in

> power. No other country has ever exploited its system of social protection in such blatant fashion and, at the same time, used it as a propaganda device. (1971, p. 245)

It is ironic that, in certain respects, the Russian social security system closely resembles that of America — this is particularly so as far as the maintenance of work incentives is concerned. Although Madison points out that provisions have been progressively liberalized since 1956 she remarks that the policy has also consistently been to, 'use the system as a work-incentive tool' (1973, p. 99). At the same time, as in America, there have been moves within recent years to reduce the costs of social security by returning certain groups — able-bodied and impotent poor alike — to the labour market. The current position, according to Madison, is that:

> the government is intensifying its efforts to draw still more adults into the labor force, both the able-bodied and the disabled and aged, and to have them remain at work for longer periods of time. (1973, p. 99)

Although the provision of benefits is determined, to some extent, by the principle of 'to each according to his need' it is also firmly governed by the principle of 'to each according to his work'. The effect of this is:

> At the present time, many official spokesmen are again stressing (as they did prior to 1956) the work-incentive potential of the social security–social insurance system. They note that its very existence is a 'moral' stimulus to work, for the individual worker. (Madison, 1973, p. 100)

A recent report in *The Times* (16.1.80) reveals that the current debate about the proper relationship between work and welfare in Russia bears striking similarities to that taking place in countries such as Britain and America. It begins:

> To refuse to work is not simply a social disgrace in the Soviet Union. It is a criminal offence which can lead to prosecution under anti-parasitic legislation.

The Russian public is said to be growing increasingly anxious about the failure to encourage the 'workshy' to find suitable employment. The newspaper *Pravda* asks:

> Isn't it about time we stopped allowing these malingerers to take advantage of the law? Should the humanity of Soviet law be used in a calculating manner to avoid working altogether?

As *The Times* report explains, the growing labour shortage in the country has led the Soviet press to devote increasing attention to a campaign to root out the 'idlers and malingerers'.

> Articles have portrayed the idle young men as sick people, filled with self-delusions, cunning parasites and spongers, protected from the penalties for the anti-social irresponsibility by indulgent wives or mothers.

Thus, it can be shown that similar (though not identical) patterns of relationship between work, welfare and control exist in societies with different economic systems, different political systems and different ideological outlooks. These illustrations have necessarily been selective and barely do justice to what is a complex web of influences. We have also left out many more examples, such as the case of Britain in the 1920s and early 1930s, which would have elaborated the theme still further. However, in characterizing the ways in which different societies have attempted to link the world of work and the world of welfare it is important to note the significance of social change. The kind of relationships we have described are not fixed and vary, from time to time, in accordance with different pressures which are brought to bear and in the light of wider social and economic changes. An important question, which remains, is to ask how and why such interconnections are formed. A number of writers, including Richard Titmuss, Peter Townsend, John Goldthorpe and Harold Wilensky, have sought to explore this issue. The revival of interest, among Marxist scholars, in the function of social welfare systems has also led to some valuable insights.

One of the most important contributions of Marxist analyses of social policy (see Saville, 1957; O'Connor, 1973; Gough, 1975; 1979) has been their emphasis on the necessity of seeing welfare activities in the context of a broad political and economic debate. While many of the early writers and 'social conscience' theorists in social policy viewed the welfare system as a discrete area of State and voluntary activity designed to relieve human suffering, Marxist writers have shown how decisions about welfare have been bound up with questions about the economy and about political stability. Mishra's characterization of 'the Marxian perspective on welfare' illustrates the interrelatedness of spheres of governmental activity which the early 'social policy perspective' assumed to be separate and unconnected.

> (1) Welfare entails the regulation of work and living conditions and the distribution of societal resources on the basis of human need. . . .
> (6) Social services make important contributions to the efficient and smooth working of the capitalist economy.
> (7) They help to mitigate class conflict and thus stabilise the social order. (Mishra, 1977, pp. 67, 76)

As Mishra points out Saville's (1957) analysis suggests that social reform in industrial society has been motivated less by philanthropic concern than by other factors, 'the case for positive social policies was often argued on the grounds of social and economic efficiency and political stability' (p. 69), and in America, too:

> the themes uppermost in the minds of the reformers were the containment of labour unrest and political instability through moderate reforms and the attainment of greater rationality and efficiency in industry. (p. 69)

The value of the Marxist (or Marxian) perspective is that, although comparisons are usually limited to study of the industrialized countries of Western Europe and North America, there is a concerted attempt to develop theory to explain the linkages between welfare and other activities, where once explanations were offered in terms of the particular conditions prevailing in individual countries or even in terms of individual political actions. Thus we can see that the view of welfare held by Bismarck in Germany was not peculiar to him and his times but was also characteristic of other countries in other periods. The pattern of relationships between work, welfare and control can — to a large extent — be shown to be features of industrial societies in general rather than one country in particular. At the same time, while this book begins from the assumption that the development of a comparative perspective can be useful in illuminating the central determinants of social policy in different societies, the Marxist approach adopts the complementary view that the inherent qualities of social policy in capitalist societies can *only* be appreciated when viewed comparatively. So, Gough, for example, argues that:

> an approach that focuses on the links between the capitalist mode and social policy must necessarily be comparative in scope, explaining the differences and similarities between countries in the Western World. (1979, p. 15)

Gough's is an important contribution to the development of comparative studies of social policy in capitalist societies. His analysis explains the complexities of the work and welfare relationships in a more detailed manner than has been possible in this section. His argument is that four sets of changes within the capitalist mode of production have given rise to important developments in social policy. Firstly, the growth of a system in which the majority of the workforce are paid employees has left the individual ill prepared to deal with such contingencies of life as old age, sickness and unemployment. 'The very condition of being paid a employee, then, exposes a family to hardship through loss of wage, for whatever reason. The development of modern social-security systems is ultimately grounded in this basic fact' (p. 33). Secondly, the rapid progress of industrialization resulting in inhuman conditions in the workplace, created conditions to which many governments saw fit to respond. Some of the first initiatives in social policy, therefore, took the form of factory regulations (governing hours and conditions of work) and workmen's compensation. Thirdly, the division of labour gave rise to the demand for new skills and more specialized education, which in many countries was a spur to the development of mass public education, and fourthly, the growth of towns created new needs for housing and public health measures. As Gough carefully emphasizes, these changes in industrial production may have been necessary but not sufficient conditions for the growth of State welfare and although many capitalist societies eventually found ways of meeting new needs there is no suggestion that the State *had to* act.

The modern welfare state, Gough argues, performs two basic functions, the first of which is 'the reproduction of labour power within capitalism'. The second is the support of non-working groups in society. 'The second role of the welfare state', however, 'cannot be sharply distinguished from the first for several reasons' (p. 47). Children who are temporarily members of the non-working group are the future working population while others who may currently be members of this group (the sick and the unemployed) may also be potentially employable. Such individuals form part of the 'reserve army of labour'. In Gough's view:

> The two basic activities of the welfare state correspond with the two basic activities in all human societies: the reproduction of the working population and the maintenance of the non-working population. The welfare state is the institutional response within advanced capitalist countries to these two requirements of all human societies. (p. 48)

Gough's conclusion leads on to another important dimension of the relationship between work and welfare which is the function of social policy in the development of an effective workforce.

Welfare and the workforce

A number of writers have argued that the primary purpose of social policy in any industrial society has been the production of a healthy and literate workforce able to fulfill the requirements of a complex economy. The development of many social services, but most obviously public education and medical care, is attributed to the need to have workers who are able — both mentally and physically — to take up their place in capitalist society. The campaign for 'national efficiency' in Britain at the end of the nineteenth century is one particularly striking example of the development of social policy for economic ends. Although the actual effects on policy of the campaign are debatable the rationale which was offered for extending social services was certainly that of economic efficiency. As Hay has observed:

> Health services would ensure that the worker was returned to the labour force as soon as possible after illness. More generally, by raising the standard of health of the community, especially among children, such services would yield an economic return outweighing their cost. Education would have similar results. (1975, pp. 16–17)

This concern with economic efficiency coincided with the discovery that large numbers of army recruits for the Boer War were unfit to fight. As a result the Interdepartmental Committee on Physical Deterioration was set up, in 1904, to investigate the claim that 'the progressive degeneration of the health of the working classes had set in' (Hay, 1975, p. 54). It recommended medical inspections of schoolchildren and also prompted the passage of the Education (Provision of Meals) Act in 1906, which provided free school meals, and the proposals for health insurance which were contained in the National Insurance Act of 1911. These and other reforms introduced by the Liberal government at the turn of the century solved both political and economic problems. Lloyd George, Churchill and others, for example:

> saw the strategic importance of welfare measures which would, at one and the same time, act as an antidote to socialism and hinder the polarisation of the electorate between Labour and Conservatives in Britain, contribute to the efficiency of the British economy by preventing the physical and mental deterioration of the workers, and provide a measure of social justice which would help to attract working class votes without alienating the middle classes. (Hay, 1975, pp. 61–2)

The seminal essay by Richard Titmuss (1976), on 'War and Social Policy' examines in more detail the effects on social policy of the demands of modern warfare. There are, he argues, three stages in the progression of interest in these matters. Firstly, there is concern about the quantity of men available to fight, secondly, there is interest in the quality of recruits and, thirdly, there is a more widespread concern for the well-being of the population as a whole, especially children, who are the next generation of recruits. In the second stage, as increasing numbers of men are rejected or invalided out of the services, other costs are incurred by the community. The outcome, Titmuss observed, is that:

> The social costs of the Boer War and the First World War, as measured by expenditure on pensions, widows' benefits, medical care, rehabilitation, sickness claims, rent subsidies and national assistance, represent a substantial proportion of the social service budget today. (p. 80)

Although Titmuss made these remarks in 1955 it is clear that they are still applicable today and the social costs of the Second World War can also be added to the sum. Obviously, this is not a phenomenon peculiar to Britain and similar developments can be found in other countries which have been engaged in warfare in this century. In America, for example, the costs of veterans' benefits (pensions and compensation, health and medical programs, education, life insurance and welfare) have risen significantly since the war in South East Asia.

Rimlinger, too, has shown how widespread is the tendency to use social policy for economic and political ends, whether it be to increase industrial productivity or to provide men for the armed services. He argues, for example, that:

> Aside from being a means to enhance welfare, social security programs also are measures that affect the quantity and quality of a country's manpower resources. The poor laws constituted a manpower policy that was fairly well suited for a time when labour was abundant and mostly unskilled. The main requirement then was the maintenance of work habits among the marginal elements of the work force. . . . As industrialization progressed, labour became not only more scarce relative to capital, but it achieved a much higher level of skill. . . . At this stage it became profitable, from the point of view of productivity, to develop and to maintain the capacity and the willingness to work. The worker's physical strength and good will had become important assets. (1971, pp. 9–10)

Rimlinger goes on to illustrate these points with reference to Russia, America, Germany and France as well as Britain. In an earlier article, in 1966, he had already indicated, how extensive was the usage of social insurance as a means of increasing efficiency, after the onset of industrialization:

> The significance of social insurance as an investment in national productivity was first emphasized in Germany, but the idea was gaining acceptance in other industrialized countries. For instance, Winston Churchill's advocacy of social insurance in the early years of the century was influenced by his recognition of the relationship between economic insecurity and national defense. This recognition was an essential ingredient also in Teddy Roosevelt's 'New Nationalism' which was much concerned with the question of national efficiency. (Rimlinger, 1966, p. 567)

Germany was held up as the shining example of what could be

achieved through social insurance. Productivity increased as a result of the improved health of workers, reduced absenteeism and lower accident rates. It was also established that invalidity insurance had spin-off effects on health insurance and medical care, as prevention was seen to be cheaper than cure. These lessons were learned not only in Western Europe and the United States, but the Soviet Union, too, saw the value of social welfare as a means of increasing productivity. Indeed Rimlinger maintains that, 'The Soviet Union, more than any other country, has used welfare programmes for the purpose of influencing labour productivity' (1966, p. 569). The problem is not to find examples of the uses of social policy as explicit means of enhancing the well-being of the workforce for the purposes of increased efficiency and productivity but to discover whether there are any exceptions to this general observation.

A final illustration of the relationship between welfare and the workforce is provided by Bowles and Gintis (1976) in their detailed account of the functions of education in capitalist societies. It is a mistake, they argue, to see this relationship simply in terms of the skills which are developed in schools and which are bought in the labour market. The process, it is suggested, goes much further and:

> To capture the economic import of education, we must relate its social structure to the forms of consciousness, interpersonal behaviour and personality it fosters and reinforces in students. (1976, p. 9)

Thus, rewards in the educational system (in the form of high grades) are seen as being related to the development of positive attitudes to work by students. Strong work orientations are fostered because they enhance the productive capacity of the worker. The patterns of authority found in the workplace are also reflected in the organization of educational institutions so that potential workers become familiar with the kind of controls which will subsequently be applied. A further function of education is to legitimize, to generate acceptance of, economic inequality. However, as Bowles and Gintis point out, education has not actually been 'a finely tuned instrument of manipulation in the hands of socially dominant groups' (p. 12) and the provision of education has sometimes been counter-productive. While, in some cases, it has produced a passive acceptance of the status quo, in others it has led to criticism of the principles of capitalism. In conclusion, therefore, while they argue that there is:

> little doubt that the US educational system works to justify economic inequality and to produce a labour force whose capacities, credentials, and consciousness are dictated in substantial measure by the requirements of profitable employment in the capitalist economy (p. 151)

they emphasize that the relationship between welfare and the workforce is not simply a technical one. The analysis offered by Bowles and Gintis, in this respect, goes much further than that of many writers who have conceived the issues in rather more simplistic terms. Although the argument is developed mostly in terms of the American system, rather than in capitalist societies in general, a number of the observations make sense in the context of other industrialized societies and it would be interesting to test out Bowles and Gintis' thesis more fully against a wider range of data.

Welfare and trade unions

One question which must be asked in tracing the origins of policy and in mapping the policy-making process in any country is 'what was the influence of different interest groups?' In the field of social policy a large number of bodies have contributed to the development of welfare programmes — politicians, ministers, civil servants, professional groups, voluntary organizations and consumers amongst others. One issue which has preoccupied historians of social policy has been to discover how far social policies resulted from pressue 'from below', from the activities of trade unions and organized labour generally as opposed to originating within government. The debate has been tied to the more theoretical questions about whether policies emerge as compromises, out of a process of conflict between different interest groups, or whether they develop on a consensual basis of rational planning at the executive level. The size and strength of working-class organization has been one factor considered by Wilensky as a determinant of social policy. His hypothesis is that, 'A large, strongly organized working class with high rates of participation in working class organizations . . . fosters pro-welfare-state ideologies and big spending' (1975, p. 65). His data from 22 'rich countries' does, he claims, support this view and that, furthermore, there is a 'snowball effect' so that highly developed welfare States (which have grown out of working-class pressure) in turn provide increased opportunities for working-class activism. This is especially so, he suggests, in Germany, France, Belgium, Sweden and Austria. Another dimension to this cumulative process is discussed by Gough (1979, chapter 7). The growth of the public sector in health, education and other social services has also meant the increase of public sector employees, and thus the expansion of an increasingly militant group with a vested interest in the development of welfare services.

We can see, from looking at comparative data, that the impact of trade unions and organized labour has varied from country to country. We can also see that the trade union movement is not a homogeneous grouping and that, within it, there is often dissension about whether to support or oppose particular social reforms.

In many respects, America is at one end of the scale of trade union participation in social policy-making (with what Heidenheimer describes as an 'amazingly low level of involvement in the planning of social security programs', (1973, p. 318)), with the Soviet Union at the other end, and Britain and most other European countries somewhere between the two. Generally speaking, trade unions in America have been relatively inactive in pursuing social reform. Indeed, in many cases, they have actually opposed it. As Heidenheimer et al. show:

> Leaders of unions were particularly opposed to sickness and unemployment insurance, largely for fear of weakening union influence over workers and increasing workers' dependence on the government. (1976, p. 196)

Although they subsequently lent support to proposals for old age pensions and unemployment insurance, many unions displayed an ambivalence to social reform movements which still persists. This position contrasted with that in many European countries (with the exception of Germany) where, after some initial opposition, unions have generally played a positive, if tentative, role. Domhoff (1971) accounts for the antagonism of American trade unions not only in terms of their concern for the possible subversion of the labour movement, but also because of their suspicion of both the paternalism of the reformers themselves and of the Government as agent of that reform.

Rimlinger draws interesting comparisons between this negative view of American trade unions and those in Germany:

> unlike British trade unions, which paid at least lip service to the idea of social security in the early days, American unions were mostly hostile. In this regard there was a striking parallel between them and the German labor movement, although at opposite ends of the ideological spectrum. The bald fact is that in both countries the labor leaders showed more concern for the welfare of their organizations than for the welfare of the working class. (1971, p. 80)

Critics have been divided in their assessment of the extent to which trade unions have actually influenced social policy. Indeed, it is very difficult in a complex process of policy development to identify any tangible changes which can be specifically attributed to the activities of one particular group, and the matter inevitably remains an open question, at least to some degree. The weighting given to the significance of this interest group, amongst others, is very much determined by the observer's ideological position and we cannot state categorically that one is obviously correct and the other wrong. Mishra, following Saville (1957), concluded that, 'the decisive influence in the development of state welfare has been that of the trade unions and the labour movement as a whole' (Mishra, 1977, p. 103), while Ginsburg, from a not dissimilar ideological basis, concludes that:

> the working class through the organs of the trade union movement and the labour Party has exerted very little 'real' as opposed to 'formal' control over the shape of welfare policy and administration. (1979, p. 10)

The fact is that we cannot easily generalize about the influence of trade unions on social policy and, in many cases, we have to conclude that it depends upon the issue and it depends upon the union. To take just one example; Hilary Land has shown that, while the labour movement as a whole was traditionally opposed to the introduction of family allowances in Britain (on the grounds that it would weaken worker solidarity) certain unions — such as the Miners' Federation — were strong supporters of a national, non-contributory benefit scheme (see Hall et al., 1975, p. 169).

However, if there is some doubt about the degree and extent of involvement of unions in policy-making and administration within the countries of Europe and North America there is no doubt that the common experiences of these countries contrast sharply with the position in the Soviet Union. In the case of Russia, trade unions play a central and, in the context of Soviet ideology, an indispensable role in the delivery of services. Both Madison (1968) and Rimlinger (1961; 1966; 1971) have pointed to the extensive participation of trade unions at a variety of levels. Further illustrations are offered by Trofimyuk (1977) who shows that, 'The Soviet trade unions administer some 12,000 health centres, boarding houses, and tourist and leisure centres, and about 35,000 pioneer camps' (p. 53). They are also involved in the provision of occupational health care which includes a comprehensive range of services concerned particularly with prevention. They are responsible for the supervision of medical services for workers, for dietary advice and for health and safety at work, employing their own inspectorate and physicians.

Trade unions are particularly active in the field of income maintenance and the All-Union Central Council of Trade Unions (AUCCTU) has overall responsibility for the administration of social insurance. Also, as Trofimyuk puts it, 'trade unions enjoy the right of initiating new legislation' (1977, p. 56). The AUCCTU draws up regulations for social insurance benefits, it advises on economic policy with respect to income maintenance and fixes the allocation of budgetary resources. Trade unions also:

> participate directly in decisions by social security bodies regarding the award of pensions and the establishment of invalidity groups; they further ensure public supervision of the correct expenditure of resources allocated to pensions protection and services for pensioners. (p. 57)

The participation of trade unions in both the making of social policy and its administration, therefore, is far more firmly built into the fabric of Russian society (as one might expect) than in the other countries referred to above. Nevertheless, the relationship between trade unions and social policy is an important one in most societies. This is no less so where trade unions play only a small part and lack of union involvement, in itself, may be a useful indication of other significant dimensions of social policy.

The 'scrounging' issue

Finally, differing attitudes to the relationship between work and welfare are often highlighted in debates about how to deal with those who abuse (or allegedly abuse) the welfare system. Conflict has centred particularly upon the treatment of the able-bodied who are out of work and dependent upon welfare. As Dennis Marsden has observed:

> Underlying the arguments about unemployment and the unemployed is a basic disagreement about the nature and meaning of work in society. To what extent can or should work be regarded as a service, not only performed by the worker for society but also made secure for the worker by the State, and subsidized if necessary? (Marsden and Duff, 1975, p. 17)

In many societies it is possible to identify a group who act as scapegoats for the ills of the welfare system and upon whom hostile attitudes are particularly focused. In Britain, for example, they are known as the 'work-shy' or 'scroungers', in America 'welfare chiselers', in Australia 'dole bludgers' and in Israel 'work-shirkers'. Hostility to these groups can be traced back to the poor laws when stigma was deliberately used as a means of rationing benefits. The principle of 'less eligibility' and the 'workhouse test' were both designed to confer shame upon the pauper seeking help and to deter others from doing the same. Inequality of treatment, under the poor laws, has had profound and lasting effects, particularly for the able-bodied poor. In America, for example, as Jacobus ten Broek's careful analyses have established, a dual system of family law has evolved which discriminates, quite specifically, against the poor on the basis of their poverty (see Handler, 1971).

In countries such as Britain and America we can see that, over a long period of time, attitudes to social policy tend to alternate between moods of reform and 'welfare backlash' or between 'witch hunt and reform' as Gronbjerg et al. (1978) put it. The periods of 'backlash' are frequently characterized by attempts to reduce public expenditure by removing the able-bodied poor from the welfare rolls, by introducing (or more strictly enforcing) work tests or work requirements, and by the desire to root out abuse and to punish those who are allegedly abusing the system — either by administrative controls or penal sanctions. Furthermore, backlash frequently occurs in periods of high unemployment when the chances of the able-bodied actually finding work are much reduced.

Deacon's work on 'scrounging' in Britain (Deacon, 1976; 1978; 1980) has illustrated the essentially cyclical nature of attitudes towards the poor and unemployed. A rapid increase in unemployment after the end of the First World War led to the introduction, in 1921, of the 'genuinely seeking work test'. Applicants for relief were required to demonstrate that they had made exhaustive attempts to find work, before they would be considered for benefits. A number of arbitrary restrictions were imposed and many able-bodied poor were denied help, even when no jobs were available. Although unemployment nationally was high, and increasing, and although stricter controls were being enforced, stories of abuse and scrounging were rife. By the mid-1970s, and in similar circumstances, the pattern was beginning to repeat itself and during 1976, public concern about scrounging and payments to the unemployed, according to Deacon, 'became more intense and was expressed more widely than at anytime since the 1920s. Allegations of scrounging received extensive coverage in the press and the response of the public to such claims became a major political issue' (1978, p. 120). Recent concern about scrounging arose out of the allegations, made in 1976, by Ian Sproat MP that 20 per cent of social security claims were fraudulent and only half those receiving unemployment benefit were actually looking for work. Subsequent investigations revealed that, although a small amount of abuse did exist, these claims were wildly exaggerated. However, the denial of abuse received considerably less publicity than the original allegations. It is clear that, in this case and others, public attitudes to scrounging are barely related to evidence of abuse. As Marsden observes, 'Of all the myths of the Welfare State, stories of the work-shy and scroungers have been the least well-founded on evidence, yet they have proved the most persistent' (Marsden and Duff, 1975, p. 17).

There is evidence from America (where negative attitudes towards the unemployed are generally harsher) that not only does public opinion bear little relationship to the facts about abuse but also that there is a resistance to information which suggests contrary explanations (Feagin, 1975, p. 122). Concern with scrounging and abuse has been a central feature of American social policy and, as we suggested earlier, it has resulted in the introduction of work requirements for benefits, work incentive programmes, the employment of large numbers of social security investigators and, in some States, the use of computerized surveillance techniques to check the financial backgrounds of claimants.

A comparative study, by Stephen Leibfried, of public assistance in the United States and Germany shows the different emphasis which the two countries place on the elimination of fraud and abuse. In Germany, he argues:

> the whole system not only puts less stress on the 'stick' (on administrative devices to enforce work) but also less on the 'carrot' (monetary work incentives). Hence reform policy takes a negative stance to a lesser degree than it does in the United States: but it is also more bureaucratized and less controversial. (Leibfried, 1978, pp. 60–1)

The negative features of American social policy are shown in a variety of ways:

> Procedures are characterized not only by indifference toward the applicant, as in West Germany, but also by strong indications of hostility. Self-policing is intensive and 'fraud campaigns' triggered by suspicious welfare officials and auditors are widespread. Continuous and routine checks on fraud through 'computer-matching', telephone 'hot lines' and checks on mismanagement through technically sophisticated management controls ('quality control' programs) are indications of active hostility toward the welfare population. (p. 61)

Leibfried shows that in California alone (a State generally regarded as liberal in its social programmes — at least until the passage of Proposition 13 in 1978) 300 special investigators were being used to detect fraud, at a cost of 7.5 million dollars. The Germans, on the other hand, claim to have no special investigators and no fraud detection squads. This leads Leibfried to conclude that California: 'with only one third of West Germany's population expends more man hours on 'hunting down welfare chiselers' than are expended in all of West Germany' (p. 74).

Public opinion polls show that a large proportion of the population are prepared to 'blame the victim' for his unemployment and poverty. One survey, by Joe Feagin, for example shows that 88 per cent of the sample felt that 'lack of thrift and proper money management' were either 'very important' or 'somewhat important' causes of poverty while 88 per cent felt that 'lack of effort by the poor themselves' was important. Eighty-four per cent agreed with the view that 'there are too many people receiving welfare money who should be working' and 71 per cent that 'many people getting welfare are not honest about their "need" ' (Feagin, 1975, chapter 4).

Many of the same points are made by Abraham Doron in his account of public assistance in Israel:

> The attitude toward public recipients is reflected by the common belief that the public assistance beneficiaries are 'work-shirkers', that is, persons capable of work but reluctant to make the effort to support themselves. This opinion is deeply entrenched among the public and prevails despite the publication of evidence that most public assistance recipients suffer from a variety of handicaps and are thus, for reasons beyond their control, incapable of supporting themselves. A survey conducted in 1970 by the Ministry of Welfare found that 37% of a representative sample of the working population reckons that the assistance payments encourage people not to work. (1978, p. 448)

Similar research has recently been conducted in the countries of the EEC with interesting results (Commission of the European Communities, 1977). It showed that the British were considerably more likely to attribute poverty to 'laziness and lack of willpower' than any other nation and that they were at least twice as likely to feel that the authorities were 'doing too much for people in poverty' than any other nation. The actual figures show that 45 per cent of the British respondents agreed with the first proposition (as compared with a low of 11 per cent in Denmark and 25 per cent in the EEC as a whole) and 20 per cent with the second (compared with 2 per cent in Italy, France and Belgium and 7 per cent in the EEC as a whole). One tentative conclusion which we might draw from these findings is that the 'scrounging' problem is much more of an issue in Britain than in any other country of the EEC. However, we would need more information than is currently available, in order to substantiate this idea fully.

The scrounging issue, therefore, is one dimension (varying in significance from one country to another) of the broader problem of how, on what basis and by whom, support should be given to the able-bodied poor. As we have indicated throughout this chapter the relationship between work and welfare is a highly complex and often ambiguous one. We have shown that, in every country discussed, social policy is not a discrete area of government activity concerned only with meeting social need and the relief of distress. On the contrary it is closely bound up with other aspects of political and economic decision-making, particularly with manpower and labour market policies. At the same time the links between the world of work and the world of welfare are more explicit at certain periods and in certain countries than others. Most observers agree, for example, that seventeenth century (and later) poor laws were specially intended to enforce controls in the labour market while students of Russian social policy concur that social policies are replete with expectations about work incentives and performance. Recent Marxist literature has been particularly helpful in elucidating the linkages between work, welfare and broader questions of the control of production, and political economy. Out of all these complex relationships one issue stands out as being of central importance — that is the question of how different societies deal with their able-bodied poor. For students looking for a starting point in their comparative research this question is one of the most meaningful and productive. In answering it, with the use of both historical and contemporary evidence, they will inevitably begin to acquire a 'feel' for the country they are considering.

CHAPTER 7

Public and Private Systems of Welfare

In the preceding chapters we have primarily been concerned with public systems of welfare, administered and financed by central and local government. We have also indicated, that these have not been the only means of meeting needs and that, beyond the public sector, there is a wide range of services and facilities provided by the Church, by voluntary organizations, trade unions and employers and private entrepreneurs. This chapter focuses particularly upon these non-State systems of welfare and looks at the ways in which they interrelate with public services. We have already noted that one of the most significant stages in the development of social policy occurs during the process of secularization, when responsibilities evolved in the private sector gradually come to be taken over by the State. But this is not a once and for all transition and many of the fiercest policy debates in industrialized societies still rage over the question of the respective contributions of public and private agencies in social welfare. Should parents be allowed to buy a superior education for their children? Would contributions towards the cost of services — school meals, prescriptions, etc. — engender a greater sense of responsibility and less abuse? Is medical care a consumption good to be bought and sold on the private market? Are the 'fringe benefits' provided by employers to their workers part of a secondary welfare system and should they be treated accordingly? Should the provision of houses be left to private enterprise or should local authorities be the main builders and providers of housing? Many of these questions bring into sharp focus the conflicting values and attitudes about the respective merits of public and private systems of care.

Until relatively recently the main orientation of studies which have examined private or non-State systems of care has been upon the contributions of voluntary organizations, charities, pressure groups and self-help groups to social welfare. Generally speaking they have been regarded as offering desirable and legitimate alternatives to public welfare. However, the main purpose of this chapter is to explore certain aspects of the hidden welfare system where the benefits to consumers are often less visible, indirect and — in some cases — of dubious legitimacy. This is the welfare system of fiscal and occupational benefits and of the purchase and sale of welfare goods and services on the private market.

Before going on to examine these issues, brief mention should be made of the undoubted significance of voluntary organizations, of various types, in the enhancement of social welfare. Such organizations have been important, historically, as forerunners to State-provided social services, they have been important cross-nationally in countries in which suspicion of government intervention has led to a search for alternative ways of meeting needs and they have been important in offering services which governments could not or would not provide. In countries such as America and Holland voluntary organizations have flourished while in others, such as Russia, they are virtually unknown.

Examination of the American case, in particular, reveals a bewildering variety of voluntary activities. There is allegedly a self-help group in America for every illness listed by the World Health Organization and branches of such organizations as Check-Cashers Anonymous, Rich Kids Anonymous and Mistresses Anonymous may be found in cities across the country. The tradition of voluntary association and self-help is long established. As de Tocqueville remarked in *Democracy in America,* which was first published in 1835, 'in no country of the world has the principle of association been more successfully used or applied to a greater multitude of objects than in America' (de Tocqueville, 1954 edn., p. 198). Charities and foundations, operating in the voluntary sector, have become big business and have been responsible for dispensing millions of dollars. According to Horowitz and Kolodney, for example:

> The income of the 596 largest tax-exempt foundations is more than twice the net earnings of the nation's 50 largest commercial banks. The annual income of the Ford Foundation alone exceeds that of the world's biggest bank and has totalled almost two billion dollars over the last 30 years. (1974, p. 43)

Even then the foundations contribute only a small proportion of the total national voluntary welfare effort. In 1974, for example, of the 25.2 million dollars raised for voluntary work 19.8 million came from contributions from individuals while only 2.1 million came from foundations, with the remainder contributed by business corporations and charitable bequests (*Social Indicators,* 1976, p. 551). It is worth noting that the figure of 25.2 million dollars roughly equalled total public expenditure on social security in Britain that year.

To give some indication of the scale of giving by foundations, in the past, Horowitz and Kolodney explain that the Ford Foundation's expenditure, in the eighteen months beginning in 1956, of 500 million dollars was, 'like giving away Time, Inc., Magnavox, General Mills, Pepsi-Cola, or even American Motors' (Horowitz and Kolodney, 1974, p. 47). Such apparent generosity, however, also resulted in considerable benefits for the foundations themselves, documented in some detail by Horowitz and Kolodney, in the form of tax concessions and the retention of assets which would otherwise have been redistributed. But an overemphasis on the role of foundations conceals the rich variety of well-intentioned voluntary work which takes place in all aspects of the health and social services. A survey in 1974, for example, showed that 23.5 per cent of the population over the age of 14 were engaged in some form of voluntary activity (Social Indicators, 1976, p. 549). This compares with a figure of only 9 per cent for Britain (Social Trends, 1979, p. 218). The voluntary sector, for a variety of reasons, therefore, is not to be ignored, but little more will be said of it in this chapter.

Many of the debates about the relative advantages of public and private welfare are based on assumptions of ideal-type systems which are either purely private or purely public. However, if we look at the experience of various countries we can see that each has a different 'mix' of both public and private systems. The question is, what determines that mix, what implications does it have for consumers and potential consumers and how does it affect the orientation of social policy in different societies? In each case the balance is always shifting, and adjustments are frequently made at the margin between public and private sectors. We need to know what the issues are at this margin and how different societies have resolved them.

First of all we need to consider more carefully how these distinctions between public and private systems may be drawn and what meaning we can attach to them.

The social division of welfare in comparative perspective

One of the most important contributions to the analysis of public and private welfare remains that of Richard Titmuss, in his seminal essay 'The Social Division of Welfare' (in Titmuss, 1976). All 'collective interventions to meet certain needs of the individual and/or to serve the wider interests of society' he argued, can be grouped broadly under three headings: 'social welfare, fiscal welfare and occupational welfare'. The important point is that:

> when we examine them in turn, it emerges that the division is not based on any fundamental difference in functions of the three systems (if they may be so described) or their declared aims. It arises from an organizational division of method which is, in turn, related to the division of labour in complex industrial societies. (Titmuss, 1976, p. 42)

Although Titmuss does not call upon detailed comparative data to illustrate this division he clearly assumes it to be applicable to industrialized societies in general and not simply to Britain. For the purposes of the present discussion it is really his second and third categories of 'fiscal' and 'occupational welfare' which are of particular interest.

Fiscal welfare frequently takes the form of income tax relief and allowances and recognizes a variety of 'states of dependency', especially in childhood and old age and in what one might describe as 'domestic service'. Evidence from other countries shows that systems of fiscal welfare are quite widely employed as an adjunct to or, in some cases, instead of social welfare benefits. Kaim-Caudle's useful analysis, for example, shows that various schemes of tax allowances and concessions are in operation — including allowances for medical expenses in Australia and Ireland, for contributions to superannuation funds in Denmark, for life insurance premiums in Austria, and premiums to hospital and medical funds in Ireland and Australia (1973, pp. 8–10). Other countries, such as Germany, make allowances for certain types of educational expenditure (p. 216) while, in many others, income tax relief is one of the foremost methods of providing financial support for dependent children. Of the ten countries which Kaim-Caudle chose to study (New Zealand, Australia, Canada, Ireland, United Kingdom, Denmark, the Netherlands, Germany, Austria and the United States) only one, Denmark, offered no tax relief for dependent children while every other country (except America) provided some form of family allowance as well as fiscal relief. The highly intricate network of benefits which can be included in the catalogue of fiscal welfare measures has generally been ignored by analysts of social policy, but as Titmuss and Kaim-Caudle show, they are no less a part of national welfare systems than more easily recognizable benefits such as medical care or housing.

The same can be said of the wide range of benefits, in many countries, which come under the heading of occupational welfare. These take the form of health services, housing, education and training as well as a variety of income maintenance programmes including pensions, sickness, disability and unemployment benefit, workmen's compensation, survivors benefits and redundancy payments. They also include travelling expenses, cars, clothing, entertainment allowances and meals — or what Americans would call the 'three Martini lunch'! Some of these are mandatory programmes and employers are compelled by the government to make provision for their workforce, while others are voluntary, and provided at the discretion of the employers or trade union involved. In a number of countries which are regarded as 'laggards' in the social welfare league (such as the United States and Japan) the private sector of welfare is often highly developed, and occupational welfare schemes are extensive. It would be wrong to assume, therefore, that such needs as are met through public expenditure in countries of Western Europe are not met at all in 'low-ranking' countries. In Japan, for example, occupational welfarc is a very significant form of provision. Mishra explains that it, 'forms a part of the traditional (feudal) paternalistic relation (familism) between the employee and the employer' (1977, p. 96). Many Japanese businesses provide some form of family allowance while, in addition:

> The Japanese employer may recognize the needs of his workers in many other ways, e.g. pensions, housing, schooling, kindergarten, hospital and health care, holidays at a beach or mountain resort, marriage allowance, a loan or financial grant in the event of illness or family misfortune.

This distinction which can be drawn between social welfare, on the one hand, and fiscal and occupational welfare, on the other, forms part of what Tussing (1974) has called the 'dual welfare system'. Although his analysis is concerned primarily with America, in so far as the 'duality' of welfare dates from seventeenth-century poor laws, it can be applied to most countries whose welfare systems have similar origins. The two systems consist of one which is:

> explicit, poorly funded, stigmatized and stigmatizing, and is directed at the poor. The other, practically unknown, is implicit, literally invisible, is non-stigmatized and non-stigmatizing, and provides vast unacknowledged benefits to the non-poor. (Tussing, 1974, p. 50)

As Tussing shows, it is the *form* of the programme rather than its content which determines whether or not it stigmatizes beneficiaries and also its legitimacy. The content and functions of fiscal and occupational welfare, then, may be very similar to that of public, social welfare systems, but they do not have the same negative associations in the public mind. Tussing also suggests that *within* the category of social welfare, distinctions are made between those who receive non-contributory assistance benefits and those receiving contributory, insurance benefits. The presentation of benefits for the non-poor, especially fiscal relief, is, he argues, such that many do not even regard themselves as receiving welfare payments. Using just one example, it is argued that tax relief on mortgages in the United States in the early 1970s cost four times as much as all the housing programmes for the poor, including 'public housing, rent supplements, assistance in purchase of homes and all others' (Tussing, 1974, p. 54) and, of course, relief was most beneficial to those on higher incomes. This phenomenon has also been well documented with respect to the British situation.

Adrian Sinfield (1978) has argued that the social division of welfare is closely related to the social division of labour and that there are great variations between different societies, both historically and cross-nationally, in the precise nature of this relationship. We might add that both are also a reflection of (and, conceivably, a cause of) different ideological values and beliefs. Thus, the emphasis in America upon the virtues of occupational welfare rather than public welfare stems, in part, from negative attitudes towards government intervention and beliefs about individual freedom, private enterprise and work. Occupational welfare within the American and British systems also forms part of what we might describe as a dual system of control. While the public welfare system, as we saw in the last chapter, clearly exerts control over the behaviour of welfare recipients by making benefits 'conditional', the private system achieves similar ends, but by different techniques (see Sinfield, 1978, p. 138). Sinfield's analysis also shows that, by using comparative data, we can discern patterns in the relative development of the different sectors of welfare over periods of time. Generally speaking, he suggests, public welfare measures are the last to evolve and have consisted of, 'extending to new groups some limited support of a kind which others have already been receiving through fiscal or occupational benefits' (p. 140). Comparative evidence suggests that, 'the development of many facilities appeared to have followed much the same pattern across a number of countries' (p. 140).

Thus we can see from the research conducted by Kaim-Caudle, Sinfield and others that the notion of a 'social division of welfare', although developed in a British context, can equally be applied to other societies. Few, if any, advanced, industrialized societies spring to mind in which such a division does not exist — although the balance between the different sectors of welfare varies quite considerably in degree. Since the majority of this (and most other) books has been devoted to the public sector of welfare the remaining sections of this chapter will look more extensively at the ways in which different private systems of welfare have been developed.

Occupational welfare: America and Japan

America and Japan are both countries in which public expenditure on social welfare remains relatively low. Wilensky, for example, places them twenty-first and twenty-second respectively in his 'league table' of social security spending (as a percentage of GNP) in twenty-two 'rich' countries (1975, pp. 30–1). However, such aggregate figures give a misleading impression. The Americans and the Japanese are not simply left to their own devices when faced with contingencies such as old age and sickness, which in other countries would ordinarily be dealt with through public systems of welfare. On the contrary, elaborate networks of services exist, ranging from subsistence level provision to the very generous and technically sophisticated. Indeed, it is precisely because private welfare has proved so satisfactory for certain groups of the population (usually professional, high-income groups) that there has been such reluctance to develop public services which these groups fear would result in a 'levelling down' of standards. An examination of private welfare systems in these two countries illustrates the point made earlier, that our assumptions about the 'normal' and 'obvious' ways of meeting needs are very much determined by cultural factors. If, in the Western European context, the 'normal' way of dealing with certain states of dependency is, for the most part, through public welfare we can see that, in Japan, and to a lesser extent America the 'normal' way of meeting need is through occupational welfare.

The facilities provided through occupational welfare systems in America cover a wide range of activities in health, housing, education and income maintenance, as well as leisure services. Furthermore, they are only one part of a highly developed welfare system which (as we shall see later) also includes programmes organized by religious bodies, voluntary agencies and philanthropic foundations. In 1973 private expenditure on social welfare amounted to 107,752 million dollars (or 7.57 per cent of GNP). It accounted for 13.5 per cent of all expenditure on income maintenance programmes, 57.9 per cent of all expenditure on health and 15.8 per cent and 12.2 per cent respectively on education and welfare (*Social Indicators*, 1976).

Miller and Roby (1970) have indicated how significant occupational benefits are for certain groups of workers. Although their figures are now somewhat dated, they do show that 'nonmonetary compensation' can account for a large proportion of the income of many highly paid professional workers. It can also contribute to increasing inequalities between such groups and low paid, badly organized workers who receive few, if any, 'fringe benefits' or payments in kind. Nonmonetary compensation is especially valuable to top executives whose money income is severely reduced through taxation, and in some cases can account for up to one quarter of their annual income (Miller and Roby, 1970, chapter 3).

Wilensky and Lebeaux (1965) suggest that occupational welfare programmes can be divided roughly into three groups: those sponsored by management, those sponsored by unions, and jointly negotiated programmes. What they describe as 'the rapid growth of welfare programs in private industry', in the 1950s, was attributable, they suggest, to:

> partial acceptance of the 'security' demands of its employees; the effective 'business unionism' of American labor; the ability of industry to support such programs, or pass on the costs in higher

> prices. . . . Individualism, religious freedom, a relatively free market economy, nonideological unionism [and] industrial wealth. (1965, p. 161)

These are at the root of private welfare activity in America.

Although spending in the private sector of welfare, as a proportion of all welfare spending, has been steadily decreasing, (from 34.7 per cent in 1960 to 26.9 per cent in 1976) the provision of occupational welfare benefits is still extensive. By the end of 1975, for example, 62.4 million people were covered for life insurance and death benefits, 58.2 million for some type of health care and 30.3 million for retirement benefits (*Social Security Bulletin*, November 1977, p. 19). As far as health programmes were concerned, these 58.2 million people were covered by almost 52,000 separate plans. As with pension schemes the various health care programmes can be divided into those involving a single employer and those covering more than one employer, as well as into those which were the subject of joint negotiation between employer and employee and those which were not. Statistics show that the majority of these plans provided benefits to workers in a single company (around 90 per cent) while more than half (55 per cent) were negotiated plans. Despite the fairly wide coverage of these plans there were considerable variations between industries and in terms of the type of protection which they offered. While the majority covered a certain proportion of hospital costs, medical costs and prescriptions, few paid for domiciliary services, preventive care, dental treatment and spectacles (*Social Security Bulletin,* March 1977, pp. 13–27). Furthermore, in some industries, such as construction, services and transportation there was no immediate cover and employees had to earn their entitlement to benefits during 'waiting periods' of varying lengths. When they did become entitled to benefits the maximum number of hospital days over which cover was extended was also more limited than in other programmes (pp. 28–33).

It should not be assumed, therefore, that the sheer volume of private enterprise in welfare necessarily means that coverage is comprehensive. On the contrary, there are many groups of workers and their dependents (usually the most needy) who do not participate in private schemes.

Social Indicators 1976 (United States Department of Commerce) shows, for example that women and blacks are less likely to be covered by pension and health schemes than men and whites. Fifty-six per cent of women are *not* in a private pension scheme (as compared with 41 per cent of men) while 37 per cent are *not* in a health scheme (compared with 20 per cent of men). Fifty per cent and 34 per cent of blacks are *not* covered by pension and health plans respectively, compared with 45 per cent and 25 per cent of whites. Similarly, coverage varies with industry, occupation, age and annual wage. A high proportion of workers in communications and public utilities (82 per cent), mining (72 per cent) and manufacturing (61 per cent) participate in pension schemes compared with relatively low proportions in other industries (trade, 35 per cent; construction, 34 per cent and services, 29 per cent). Although there is a higher overall coverage in health programmes, participation is also disproportionately spread over different industries. As one might expect from these figures, white-collar and blue-collar workers are far more likely to be in pension and health schemes than service workers and farm workers. Only 24 per cent of service workers and 7 per cent of farm workers are eligible to receive private pensions, and only 45 per cent and 23 per cent respectively are covered by health insurance. The figures also show that the younger and older age groups (under 25 years and over 60) are less likely to be covered than the middle age groups. Finally, the likelihood of participation in private pension and health programmes declines dramatically with income. Sixty-six per cent of those earning less than $5,000 a year were not covered for pensions and 41 per cent were not covered by private health insurance. This brief summary shows, therefore, that the benefits of private welfare systems are very unevenly spread across potential groups in need; with the most needy receiving the least coverage.

In an essay on private pensions in the United States, Merton Bernstein (1973) explains that although such benefits were introduced from the 1880s onwards, it is only in recent years that they have ceased to be 'a matter of employers' noblesse oblige, unenforceable and unfunded' (p. 2). It was during the 1940s that systematic attempts were first made to place private pension schemes on a more stable footing:

> Unions and their members prospered as never before during that period. Faced with the retirement of elderly members on the pittance provided by Social Security, the largest and most powerful unions — the mine, steel and auto workers — pressed for private pensions through collectively bargained plans. (p. 2)

Many of the larger employers resisted these moves but, despite some early setbacks, the unions eventually prevailed. There are now more than 34,000 plans currently in operation. The majority of these schemes (around 80 per cent) are what Bernstein describes as 'single-employer plans' and there are consequent limitations on funding, coverage and transferability of pension rights. The fact that many of the pension schemes are now orientated more towards the needs of the employer than the employee leads to other serious shortcomings for beneficiaries, some of which Bernstein describes as 'scandalous'. The result has been that:

> The incentives for employers, unions and the pension industry all militate against sound plans, something which makes a dubious vehicle for reaching socially desirable results. (p. 10)

Other income maintenance programmes have been operated on similar principles, with similar outcomes. Workmen's compensation, for example, has been largely a matter for private enterprise. Some States have required employers to provide insurance for their workers, either through their own resources or with private insurance companies. The result has been inadequate compensation for loss of wages and inefficient administration of benefits. The conclusion drawn by one writer is that 'Workman's Compensation, as an instrument of social policy and measured against its own objectives as a wage replacement programme, is a disaster' (Chambers, 1975, p. 339). There are clearly limitations, therefore, to the occupational sector of welfare, both with respect to income maintenance benefits and health insurance. The problems are normally those of lack of coverage, inadequacy of benefits and inequality between workers.

If occupational welfare in the American system is essentially the 'junior partner' (however influential) in the public and private welfare business, in Japan the reverse is true. Occupational benefits are generally operating as the 'normal' and 'first-line' provision for Japanese workers and their dependents. Those public welfare facilities (and they are now quite numerous), which have developed, still tend to perform a subsidiary or 'residual' function. This is partly due to the fact that there is a stronger bond between employer and employee than is the case in most European countries. As Woodsworth put it: 'loyalty to the firm, with mutual duties and rewards, is the central dynamic of modern Japan' (1977, p. 95). The Japanese worker would often expect to spend the whole of his working life with one firm and he is bound to his employer as much through social expectations as economic ones. As Robson explains:

> the employees personal affairs are not so remote from his working life as they are in the West. The owner or manager of a firm will be a highly honoured guest at the wedding of a member of his staff. A great many social entertainments for employees are organised and paid for by the firm. (1976, p. 92)

In such a setting, therefore, the notion of occupational welfare takes on a new meaning and assumes a much greater importance than is often the case in Europe. In a large organization it can mean the prospect of permanent employment as well as a company house (or at the very least, accommodation in a company dormitory), a company pension, holidays at the company resort in the mountains or by the sea, recreational facilities, bonuses, gifts and parties. One of the best ways of illustrating the significance of the differences between European and Japanese models of occupational welfare is probably through the use of case studies. Ronald Dore (1973) has offered one such comparison of factory life in Britain and Japan. In his study of two English Electric factories and two Hitachi factories he is able to highlight a number of interesting contrasts.

As far as pension schemes are concerned, Hitachi makes more generous provision for its workers than English Electric and from an earlier retirement age. A State scheme of contributory old age pensions in Japan was not introduced until the war and the first comprehensive 'social pension system' was only established in 1961. Consequently, the burden of providing income maintenance programmes for the elderly fell primarily upon employers. One of the most striking differences between Japanese and British provision, however, in Dore's study was in housing. The Bradford English Electric factory had only 27 houses and flats available for its employees (and then on a temporary basis) in contrast with the Furusato Hitachi factory which provided enough accommodation to house all the unmarried men and women high school and university graduates. This was in addition to a company estate which housed 40 per cent of the married male employees, and low interest loans available to employees wishing to buy houses on a company plot. The overall differences between Japanese and British provision are illustrated by Dore's comment that:

> Hitachi Company's total expenditure on housing, medical

> services, canteens, transport subsidies, sports and social facilities, and special welfare grants other than pay during sickness, amounted to 8.5 per cent of total labor costs. English Electric figures are not available, but for the median British firm of a group surveyed in 1968, the corresponding figure was 2.5%, *including* sick pay. (1973, p. 203)

Different levels of expenditure, of course, reflect different attitudes towards the role of occupational welfare. As Dore observes, the Bradford factory took the view that 'a man's housing is his own affair' (p. 203) while Hitachi operated on the principle that 'the company must take the prime responsibility'. At the same time the British firm, unlike Hitachi, attached 'no great positive value to its welfare and fringe benefits' (p. 204).

Another important difference which Dore detected, was in the involvement of trade unions in welfare issues. The unions in the British factories concerned were 'completely uninvolved' (p. 207), whereas the unions in the Hitachi factories played an important role as pressure groups and in the provision of welfare facilities. They not only pressed the company to provide higher wages and better benefits but they also ran rival clubs, social facilities and loan schemes. As a matter of principle the Japanese unions contended that company welfare was 'part of the rights of employees to be guarded and extended' (p. 208).

Finally, certain differences in attitude towards the family, and its relationship with the firm, were apparent. The position in the British factories was that a man's family 'is his own concern and responsibility' (p. 209). In the Japanese factories, on the other hand, 'the long arm of the company's concern reaches further' (p. 209):

> A man's family are peripheral members of the company family. The company, for instance, offers a system of educational loans for employees' children, and maintains a dormitory in Tokyo for the children of employees attending universities or cram schools preparing for university entrance.

In addition the Mututal Aid Fund provided wedding presents, gifts on the birth of a child, on its first day in primary school and on its marriage. Gifts of condolence were also offered to workers on the death of members of their family, or in cases of flood and fire damage.

These few examples offered by Dore serve to illustrate the extent of occupational welfare within Japan and the commitment to it, as a primary source of care, by employers and employees alike. The employer has an incentive to provide benefits which will improve productivity and worker efficiency, enhance labour relations and reduce industrial conflict. The employee, in the face of under-developed State systems of welfare, can see occupational welfare as his only recourse.

It is also true that, in Japan (as in America) the benefits of occupational welfare are concentrated disproportionately upon certain groups of workers. Generally speaking, men have considerably higher wages and better occupational welfare benefits than women. At the same time, employees of large firms do substantially better in both respects than workers in small firms. Because wages are lower in small firms, their employees are more likely to need the extra resources provided by occupational welfare schemes, but they are also less likely to receive them. For example, 93.9 per cent of employees, in firms with more than 5,000 workers, lived in company houses as compared with 42.2 per cent in firms with less than 99 employees. Similarly, 98.8 per cent of employees in the first category received a health insurance supplement, compared with only 14.8 per cent in the latter (Woodsworth, 1977, p. 128). There is also inequality between occupational groups, with workers employed on a seasonal basis, in, say, agriculture and forestry being least likely to benefit. Occupational benefits are particularly good in mining, where welfare costs (as a percentage of pay) amounted to 22 per cent in 1973. Workers in the textile industry (14.6 per cent) and in the metal industry (13.1 per cent) ranked next highest (Woodsworth, 1977, p. 124). Inequalities in the workplace are also carried through into inequalities in non-working life, because benefit levels are normally calculated on the basis of work record and previous wage. For those outside the workforce — women, the unemployed or casual workers — income support is especially meagre.

Occupational welfare benefits (although they exist in countries with sophisticated and comprehensive systems of State welfare) can, therefore, be seen to have even greater significance where the links between the worker and his employment are of paramount importance. If the fiscal and occupational sectors of welfare are regarded as playing a subsidiary role in Western Europe (and, to some extent in America), we can see that the reverse is true in Japan. However, although there is no large-scale convergence between Japan and the West on this issue, it is true that the

Japanese are beginning to develop their public sector of welfare more systematically, while the fiscal and occupational sectors of welfare in the West have tended to experience a 'boom' in recent years. This is especially noticeable, for example, in the increasing interest in private health insurance in Britain.

The private market in welfare

If fiscal and occupational benefits are two components of private welfare systems, another feature of the private market in welfare consists in the buying and selling of goods and services, such as medical care, education and housing, either through insurance schemes or through direct payments by the consumer. Many of the controversies about the delivery of welfare services are concentrated upon the borderline between public welfare and this particular area of the private market. There are a number of aspects to the debate — whether the consumer should pay charges (to raise revenue and to reduce waste and abuse of the service), if so, at what level (should charges reflect the economic cost of the goods or service or should there be a subsidy?). There is the problem, on the one hand, of whether services offered in the public sector (in Britain, for example, school meals and milk, drugs and dental care) should be returned to the private market (what Gough (1979) calls the 'reprivatisation' of the welfare State) and, on the other, whether responsibilities evolved in the private sector (health care services in America, for example) should be transferred to the public sector. Conflict over the respective merits of public and private systems of care, in different countries, frequently highlights some of the issues raised in earlier chapters of this book — for example, views about the proper role of the State, attitudes towards *laissez-faire,* choice and the freedom of the individual, and the relationship between contribution (either through work or insurance premiums) and the receipt of benefits, as well as the way in which the notions of need and desert shall be applied.

One of the most useful pieces of comparative research to have explored these questions is Richard Titmuss's study of blood donation in Britain, the United States, Russia, South Africa and Japan. He is concerned, he explains:

> to examine in depth and on a comparative basis the issues of freedom of choice, uncertainty and unpredictability, quality, safety, efficiency and effectiveness and to relate such issues to the supply and distribution of human blood. (1973, p. 179)

As Titmuss shows many of the problems involved in the provision of blood are those, in microcosm, of other areas of social policy, in a variety of national contexts. In particular, there is the question of whether the distribution of blood should be governed by economic criteria or whether other criteria are more appropriate. There is also the question of whether blood is a consumption good like any other bought and sold on the private market. In the American case, payment to blood donors is defended on the grounds that it allegedly improves services, and increases the supply of blood. Competition and the pursuit of profit, it is argued, lead to greater efficiency and higher standards of care. Similarly, financial inducements to donors in Britain are advocated as a means of improving productivity and of increasing the availability of blood.

A survey of 27 countries in the 1960s revealed striking variations in practice with respect to the payment of donors. Only Britain, Eire and 'two or three other countries in the world' (p. 199) offered no payment to donors, while at the other extreme there were countries such as Sweden and the United Arab Republic in which 100 per cent of donors were paid. Japan and Germany were not far behind with 98 per cent and 85 per cent respectively. Most countries had a mix, of varying proportions of paid and voluntary donations. In some countries payment was made in kind, rather than cash, and donors were given days off work, free holidays or priority in medical treatment and housing.

Titmuss's study is important for several reasons. Firstly, it tests out, on a comparative basis, the claims that are made for the private market in welfare, in terms of its efficiency and the quality of care and freedom of choice it offers. Titmuss shows that, as far as economic efficiency is concerned, 'It is highly wasteful of blood, shortages, chronic and acute, characterize the demand and supply position and make illusory the concept of equilibrium.' Furthermore, it is administratively inefficient, 'the so-called pluralism of the American market results in more bureaucratization, avalanches of paper and bills, and much greater administrative, accounting and computer over-heads' (p. 232).

The notion that the private market, through competition, will always produce better standards of care is also shown to be questionable. Titmuss claims that blood banks in which donors are paid are far more likely to obtain and distribute contaminated blood. Research in both Japan and America showed that the typical donor frequently had little or no income and was therefore very dependent upon the payments he received from giving blood. There was also a high incidence of drug addiction, alcoholism, malnourishment and hepatitis amongst donors, and they often gave blood too frequently. The effect was that patients receiving blood from paid donors faced much greater risks of disease and death from serum hepatitis than did those receiving blood from unpaid donors.

For these and other reasons, Titmuss concluded that the consumer in the private market was considerably less free than his counterpart receiving aid from non-market sources:

> In commercial blood markets the consumer is not king. He has less freedom to live unharmed; little choice of determining price; is more subject to shortages in supply; is less free from bureaucratization; has fewer opportunities to express altruism; and exercises fewer checks and controls in relation to consumption, quality and external costs. Far from being sovereign, he is often exploited. (p. 233)

Secondly, this study is important in illustrating the effects of different social and cultural factors as determinants of social policy. Public programmes, as we indicated in chapter 3, do not spring, spontaneously, from fountains of good will or from philanthropic gestures on the part of politicians or civil servants. On the contrary, they are often fought over long and hard and frequently emerge out of compromises between different interest groups. Titmuss is careful to emphasize that the blood donor system in any country is not a discrete area of policy unaffected by external constraints. It is not simply a reflection of the whims of individual donors but its nature is governed by an intricate web of influences in the wider society. As Titmuss points out, in order to understand the significance of different blood donation practices, it is important to examine, 'the fabric of values, social, economic and political, within which acts of giving, rewarding, compelling or selling take place' (p. 202). Although some blood donors are clearly motivated by feelings of altruism, others give blood for different reasons. Titmuss found that, in America, a high proportion of donors (approximately 80 per cent) gave blood either because of the financial inducement or because they were 'tied by contracts of various kinds' (p. 108). In other words they had to 'repay' blood which they had used themselves or they had to 'pay in' to a blood bank so that, if necessary, they or their families could draw upon it at a later date. A large number of what Titmuss calls 'fringe-benefit donors' (p. 100) were found in Russia, Eastern Europe, Latin America and some African countries. Here donors were motivated by the prospect of benefits in kind and special privileges. In contrast to both these groups were the voluntary, unpaid, donors found in the British system who were motivated by altruism, reciprocity, duty and a 'general desire to help people'. Only 1.8 per cent of the respondents admitted to giving blood 'in order to obtain some benefit' (p. 264) and even then the benefit was usually an improvement in the physical health of the donor. The real question for Titmuss was how to explain these radical differences in outlook across different societies. His conclusion was that it was the societal context which determined individual behaviour — various factors such as race in South Africa, and the structure of other sectors of the health service influenced the attitudes of donors and the way in which the blood donor service was organized.

A third contribution which Titmuss makes is to highlight the point, which we have emphasized throughout this book, that although industrialized societies face common policy problems (in this case, how to procure and distribute human blood) they have resolved them in strikingly different ways. The assumption that all societies as they become more advanced grow increasingly alike in their response to social need is not borne out by comparative research. Titmuss observes that although:

> there are some who argue from theories of political and economic convergence that we are today approaching the end of the ideological debate; within Britain and other Western societies. . . . This study, in one small sector of human affairs, disputes both the death of ideology and the philistine resurrection of economic man in social policy. (p. 18)

Titmuss's study of blood donor systems, like much of the other comparative research we have referred to, indicates that what is notable about social policies cross-nationally is their differences as much as their similarities. Thus, *The gift relationship* is a useful case study in the examination of several key issues in social policy, cross-nationally. However, the book is not without its critics, especially amongst economists, and it has been shown to have some weaknesses (see Reisman, 1978; Room, 1979). As well as illustrating many of the benefits of comparative analysis, therefore, it also underlines some of its limitations.

One of the important determinants of whether a private market in welfare exists in any society, and what form it takes, is the socio-economic organization of that society. We would expect to find that the private market was more likely to flourish in capitalist societies, under liberal-democratic regimes and conservative governments than in communist or socialist societies. However, although this criterion is a useful, general indicator we should not be too ready to assume that *all* capitalist societies or *all* communist societies necessarily adopt similar practices. The research on blood donation, for example, showed that policies in America were very different from those in Britain, while the Swedish approach was different again. At the same time, Russia and America both had similar proportions (approximately 50 per cent) of paid donors. The significant difference between the operation of blood donor programmes in these two countries, however, was that, 'whereas in the United States a profit is made in the blood market by commercial concerns there is apparently no profit on the transaction in the Soviet Union' (Titmuss, 1973, p. 202). We must bear these qualifications in mind, therefore, when we say that — generally speaking — private markets in welfare, though not unknown in communist societies, are most highly developed in capitalist societies.

In most areas of social policy in Russia the private market is largely absent. Mishra's summary of the main trends in the different services reveals the following pattern:

> Unlike in capitalist countries, there are no high status, exclusive, private schools catering for the elite's children. All children attend state schools which are generally run on comprehensive, i.e. non-selective, lines. Similarly all medical care is nationalised, although private practice is allowed. Thus a doctor may be consulted on a private basis but there are no private nursing homes, hospitals or beds. . . . In housing, owner-occupation exists alongside municipal and other forms of public provision. But owner-occupation is more a legacy of the past than a form of new 'capitalism'. (1977, p. 129)

As Michael Ryan, in his study of Soviet medical care, suggests, any extensive private market in health services would be antithetical to Russian values.

> Given the ideological basis of the Soviet state it is hardly necessary to make the point that the USSR contains no health care facilities provided by private owners or by religious and philanthropic organizations, such as coexist with the British health service. (1978, p. 8)

Although a significant proportion of medical treatment is given in the workplace these occupational provisions differ from most of those described above in the sense that they are usually the responsibility of the Ministry of Health, rather than of individual employers or firms, even though the employers may have contributed to their establishment in the first place. However, it would be wrong to suggest that there is no element of 'privatism' in the Soviet medical care system. Charges are, in fact, made for drugs dispensed to out-patients, and certain dental and opthalmic services involve small costs to the patients. Similarly, convalescent care in a nursing home, or its equivalent, may be the subject of charges. As in Britain, there are exemptions for certain classes of the population — in this case young children, veterans and patients with specified chronic illnesses. Another exception to the general rule about equality of treatment in medical care is the availability of special facilities for Party members, certain occupational groups and government officials. Although in practice a significant degree of privatism and inequality exists, in principle, there is intense opposition to private markets in medicine. As Ryan comments:

> official ideology is entirely hostile to the concept of a market in medical care. Indeed the existence in other countries of private practice on a large scale receives condemnation as a hallmark of capitalist society where man exploits man and where, to quote a propaganda phrase 'medicine is business'. (p. 30)

In general, therefore, Russia is one example of a country in which the welfare system is almost entirely a public responsibility. This is especially so in medical care and it offers a distinct contrast with the American system, at the other extreme, in which — of the overall expenditure on health care in 1975 — 60.3 per cent came from private sources. (Social Indicators, 1976, p. 204). Direct payments by patients accounted for 32.6 per cent of all expenditure, private health insurance for 26.5 per cent and private philanthropy and industry for 1.2 per cent. This high level of private involvement is, in fact, a substantial reduction on the position obtaining in the early 1960s before the introduction of the limited public medical care schemes, Medicare and Medicaid (which were approved in 1965). In 1960, for example, private payments accounted for 78.3 per cent of expenditure on health, while in 1965 they accounted for 79.2 per cent of the total. Public subsidies are concentrated in particular sectors of the health service so that, whereas only 45 per cent of hospital costs are paid from private sources, 73.5 per cent of physicians fees and 94.4 per cent of dental charges are paid for privately and 91.4 per cent of the charges for drugs. What is more the Americans have fiercely defended their medical care system against the encroachment of State involvement. The first proposal for public national health insurance was introduced in Congress in 1912 by Theodore Roosevelt. At the time of writing (early 1980) no such scheme has yet been accepted.

Countries, even advanced affluent industrialized countries, therefore, differ markedly in their attitudes to private markets in welfare. In all countries there is some mix of public and private care and no country has a totally 'pure' system of either kind. The varieties of 'mix' and, to some extent, the ingredients of the mixture are very diverse. The task for the student engaged in comparative study is, firstly, to determine roughly what proportion of funds and services derive from public and private sources and secondly, to investigate what factors have produced the particular mix in any country. He/she should also consider what factors lead to a change in the balance between public and private sectors.

'Welfare backlash' and the 'reprivatization' of the welfare State

Finally, one of the most significant developments in social policy in the 1970s has been the widespread incidence of 'tax revolts' and what is generally known as 'the welfare backlash'. The debates surrounding these issues underline the critical importance of the relationship between public and private sectors of welfare and the constantly shifting boundary between the two. They are of particular interest to the student of comparative social policy because they are not confined to one national context but have arisen in several different countries. Gough (1979) has speculated that the outcome of these trends will be an increasing reliance on private markets in welfare and a 'reprivatization' of the welfare State (p. 140).

The notion of 'welfare backlash' has been particularly associated with the United States after the passage in California, in the summer of 1978, of a tax-cutting amendment to the State constitution known as Proposition 13. It was followed by the introduction, in rapid succession, of a series of similar proposals in many other States. However, as Wilensky (1975; 1976) has indicated, such developments have become a familiar phenomenon in many industrialized nations. The cross-national analysis of welfare backlash has only begun, in earnest, in the last five years so that many of the conclusions are necessarily speculative and there has been little opportunity to observe long-term developments. Nevertheless, a number of trends do seem to be emerging and suggest some of the outlines of future scenarios.

Using a number of criteria Wilensky (1976) has attempted to rank 19 advanced countries in terms of their experience of 'tax-welfare backlash'. At the top of the list come Denmark, the United States and United Kingdom and Switzerland, with 'scores' ranging from 55 to 43; in the second group are Canada, Norway, France and Finland with 36 to 32 points while, in the final group (all with relatively little experience of welfare backlash) are West Germany, Austria, Ireland and Japan on 20 points each. The kind of gross calculations which Wilensky made may lead one to regard this 'league table' with a degree of caution. However, there is some evidence to suggest that the countries which rank high in the list have experienced a greater than average level of conflict over taxes and welfare spending. This has manifest itself in a number of ways.

In Denmark in 1973 the Progress Party led by Mogens Glistrup won unprecedented electoral support and emerged as the second largest parliamentary party. Glistrup's manifesto included promises to abolish income tax by 1980; to radically reduce bureaucratic power; to abolish the welfare system and introduce (in each community) 'social guards' who would have control of limited funds and would exercise discretion over how they were spent and finally to cut the pensions of public employees and raise those of every other group. Similar developments took place in California in 1978 when 75-year-old veteran campaigner Howard Jarvis was successful in pushing through Proposition 13, an amendment to the State constitution. Jarvis, described by the press as 'the Moses of the middle classes' and representing the United Organization of Taxpayers, claimed that socialism created slavery and that, as far as he was concerned it was 'capitalism first, last and always'. Proposition 13 resulted in a 57 per cent reduction in property taxes, saving 7 billion dollars, and accompanied by the loss of 102,000 public service jobs. Meanwhile, in Britain, a series of cuts in public expenditure beginning in 1973 (and particularly directed at the social services) meant a reduction in the rate of growth in the welfare system and strongly suggest a contraction in the future. The successful election campaign which resulted in the return to power of a Conservative government in May 1979 was fought partly on a commitment to reducing income tax and also to reducing public expenditure on social welfare. A recent survey conducted by the European Commission also indicates that public opinion towards the poor and towards welfare spending is significantly more negative in Britain than in most of the other Common Market countries. Of the sample, for example, 45 per cent felt that laziness and lack of will-power were the main cause of poverty — this was a higher percentage than in any other country, while the Community average was 25 per cent. Twenty per cent of the sample also felt that 'the authorities were doing too much' to help people in poverty, this was twice the percentage in every other country and much higher than the Community average of 7 per cent (Commission of the European Communities, 1977, pp. 70–7).

Wilensky examined a number of variables in an attempt to account for the different degrees of welfare backlash in the countries in his study. His main conclusion was that, 'spending that is profligate or lean, taxing that is heavy or light, treatment of the poor that is generous or stingy have only a little to do with political fallout' (1976, p. 15). Welfare backlash, then, could not simply be seen as a reaction against high public expenditure and high levels of taxation and it was not necessarily found just in countries which had traditionally been punitive towards the poor. Wilensky claimed that, in fact, it was related to the speed at which public expenditure increased. Sudden and rapid increases in spending in countries such as the United States and Denmark (and to a lesser extent Norway and Finland) aroused alarm, and calls for a halt to public expenditure on social welfare. In countries such as Sweden, France and Germany, the steadier growth rate produced less anxiety and less political opposition. A second factor which frequently resulted in backlash was the high visibility of taxation in certain countries. Visible taxes, in Wilensky's terms, included personal income tax, property tax and wealth and gift taxes. These forms of raising revenue were contrasted with 'less visible' and 'non-visible' taxes which included sales and value added taxes (in the first group) and corporate and profit taxes and payroll taxes (in the second). Denmark, the United Kingdom and United States and Switzerland all favoured visible taxes and these accounted for a substantial proportion of tax revenue (around or somewhat above 40 per cent), while in the group of countries with little experience of welfare backlash visible taxes accounted, in most cases, for much less than 30 per cent of the total. Beyond these two sets of relatively simple indicators (rate of spending increase and visibility of taxation) the factors leading to welfare backlash became more complex and more ambiguous. Generally speaking, a high degree of governmental centralization tends to mean less backlash while the extent of social heterogeneity and the size and strength of the working class do not appear to be relevant determinants. However, there are exceptions to this general observation, Britain being an obvious example — where a relatively high degree of centralization is combined with a significant experience of backlash.

Heidenheimer et al. (1976) have identified a further feature of the American welfare system which has probably increased the incidence of backlash, this is the tendency towards the development of 'categorical' programmes for particular groups in need, rather than universal and comprehensive programmes. The effect is that 'America makes its public assistance clientele stand out conspicuously'. They are more visible and easier to attack. The problem is exacerbated by the fact that a high proportion of welfare beneficiaries are also black or hispanic and therefore visible in a more literal sense. The end result is that, 'since racial minorities are overrepresented among the poorest, the visibility of public assistance — and the potential for welfare backlash — is even greater' (1976, p. 279). A number of European countries also have categorical programmes for the needy, but Heidenheimer et al. argue that the effects are less severe in those countries because they offer benefits within the context of 'more general, population-wide forms of government support' (p. 279).

The important question here is 'what will be the outcome, both in the short and long term, of tax revolts and welfare backlash? Gough has argued that, in Britain at least, they will probably lead to a restructuring, rather than a dismantling, of the welfare State. The capitalist State, he suggests, will increasingly adapt social policies in ways which will, more specifically, serve the needs of capital. For instance, 'education and social security policies in particular can be adjusted to adapt the labour force and potential labour force more effectively to the needs of the labour market' (1979, p. 138). In practice, this may mean a movement away from the 'liberal' and 'progressive' teaching methods, introduced in recent years and a trend towards the development of the educational system for vocational and industrial training purposes. Similarly, there is likely to be an increasing emphasis in the social security system on maintaining incentives to work. This will mean more widespread usage of the kind of administrative work enforcement techniques discussed in the last chapter. It may also mean a return to 'less eligibility' as a guiding principle of social policy, and to attempts to deter potential claimants from seeking State benefits by keeping benefit levels low and by stigmatizing those who accept them. At the same time we are likely to see a reduction of certain services under the guise of 'efficiency' and 'rationality' and the replacement of personal services by more mechanical and impersonal forms of care (pp. 139–40).

Gough's predictions are given added plausibility when one considers the developments which have been taking place in the United States. Without suggesting that everything America does Britain does 5 or 10 years later we can nevertheless see a similarity in trends in social policy and a tendency for Britain to replicate the American experience. Obviously, America is starting from a very different policy heritage, but we can see at the present time many of the developments, which Gough predicts will occur in Britain. We suggested, for example, in the last chapter that the desire to maintain the work ethic has been a dominant influence on American social policy for many years. It came particularly to the fore in 1967 (partly as a reaction against the liberal years of 1964–7) and was a central feature of both Nixon's and Carter's planned social programmes. There has also been a striking tendency towards mechanization and computerization of the welfare system, quite explicitly designed to expose fraud and root out abuse. As in Britain, the estimated amount of abuse by claimants themselves is actually very low but within the administration of the services there are substantial losses and a high level of misuse of funds by administrators. One of Carter's main promises, when he came to office, was that he would eliminate mismanagement at all levels of government and would introduce more efficient and rational systems of administration. The indications are that, where this policy has been followed through, it has often led to reduced services for the consumer and to more impersonal forms of care. The other obvious effect of welfare backlash in the United States has been the closure of hospitals, schools and residential institutions for groups such as the elderly. There has been a reduction in the provision of 'public utilities' such as fire, police and rubbish disposal and the introduction of charges for some previously free facilities such as libraries, museums and leisure activities. Overall, there is strong evidence of what S.M. Miller (1978; 1979) has termed 'the re-capitalization of capitalism'. He argues that:

> the aim is to contract the public sector and thereby reduce taxation on better-off people and wealthy corporations, in order

to promote private savings and investments which are the presumed source of growth, employment and productivity. Funds for social purposes are the victims of this economic strategy. Inflation and energy issues take precedence. Oil problems are now 'the moral equivalent of war not poverty.' (1979, p. 247)

The eventual outcome of backlash which Gough foresees is what he describes as the 'reprivatisation' of the welfare State which, in a sense, is one dimension of the 're-capitalisation of capitalism'. In other words, we can expect expenditure to, 'switch from direct state provision of services to public subsidisation and purchase of privately-produced services' (p. 140). However, it would be misleading to imply that change in social policy is linear in nature. Many of the developments which Gough and others envisage are not necessarily final and immutable. Historical evidence tends to suggest much more of a 'see-saw' effect in the dominant ideologies of social policy.

Another aspect of reprivatization, which Gough does not fully discuss, would be the expansion of private markets in welfare where consumers would buy services such as education and medical care, and goods such as drugs or housing, but without necessarily having the benefit of public subsidies. The Conservative government, elected in 1979, certainly professes support for such policies. It is proposed to extend the private sectors in education, health and other fields, to reduce public subsidies for other services and to introduce or reintroduce charges for certain facilities and to abolish benefits such as death grants and maternity grants. Even assuming that only a proportion of these proposals actually come to fruition, this will still represent substantial movement towards the reprivatization of the welfare State.

However, it would be wrong to imply that we can anticipate a single-minded and unchecked march along the road to privatism. As Gough observed, some of the tendencies towards reprivatization of the welfare State may be modified in response to trade union, working-class and other interest group pressure. Heidenheimer et al. (1976) have argued, even more forcefully, that the trends outlined above may well be short-lived. Any suggestion of protracted backlash effects, they claim, 'badly misrepresents the long-term issues of social policy'. First of all, they argue, it will become clear that — contrary to popular expectation — any contraction of public programmes will actually cost money. 'Even a policy of government non-intervention', they point out, requires 'very careful planning and continuous attention by public policy makers'. The great weakness of proponents of reprivatization may prove to be that, 'like those who would only expand, those who would only cut back on social programs disregard the costs associated with the action' (p. 276). Only time will tell whether backlash and the effects of backlash will have permanent effects upon the welfare systems of industrialized societies. Contrary to the somewhat more optimistic projections of Heidenheimer et al. the indications offered by Gough, Miller and others suggest more lasting damage to the principles and practices of public welfare. Heidenheimer et al. are surely wrong in their contention that:

> the frontiers of European and American social policy are not a combat zone between pro- and anti-welfare state forces because, in practice, there is no defensible line between the armies. (p. 276)

They are, of course, right to point out that public and private systems of welfare are so closely interrelated in some respects, that it is often difficult to distinguish between the functions and effects which each has. However, even though combatants may not always be clear who the enemy is or where he/she is, or even who is in whose army, they are fighting nevertheless. As we have argued throughout this chapter, the borderline between public and private systems of care, however difficult to discern, is highly sensitive and is very much the battleground for some of the critical debates in social policy. Our reaction should not be to ignore it, simply because we cannot see it clearly but it should be to devote more attention to teasing out the complexities and interrelationships so that we can understand, more precisely, the relative contributions, to social welfare, of public and private systems and the beneficiaries they serve. Comparative research can help us to accomplish this task.

In conclusion, a comparative perspective in social policy shows that it is increasingly inappropriate to examine public welfare in isolation from other systems of care. Decisions taken in the private sector of welfare frequently have repercussions for the public sector and vice versa. In essence, both are meeting similar human needs but from different sources and for different groups of the population. The existence of dual welfare systems, involving what has sometimes been characterized as 'socialism for the rich and private enterprise for the poor' has been shown in a number of countries, especially (though not exclusively) in capitalist societies. Many current debates in industrialized countries relate to problems about the public/private dichotomy about where to draw the line between the two sectors and about the legitimacy and extent of State involvement in social welfare. Comparative research reveals an endless variety of solutions to these problems and considerable variations in the 'mix' of the public and private systems. Ultimately, it becomes very difficult to justify comparative research in social policy which does not give attention to both systems of care and equally, a satisfactory analysis of public and private welfare cannot proceed without introducing comparative data.

CHAPTER 8

Conclusion

The purpose of this book has been to show that comparative research is not simply a frill around the social policy cake, of interest only to the particularly energetic or the slightly eccentric. On the contrary, it is an important methodological tool for exploring key issues in social policy. As we have shown in earlier chapters, a number of trends and problems transcend national boundaries and it is increasingly clear that we cannot understand developments in one country in isolation from those in others. Despite the wide variety of approaches to comparison in social policy, which we identified in chapter 2, and the volume of work in this area, the systematic use of comparative methodology in policy studies is still underdeveloped. There is little doubt, however, that a greater concentration upon this line of approach would advance considerably the study of social policy both within and between different national contexts. The alternative is theory and practice, in social policy, which is stultified and introspective. Advocacy of comparative research is, in a sense, the social scientific equivalent of claiming that 'travel broadens the mind'. Comparative research in social policy broadens the mind, too, by overcoming the tendency, in policy studies, to be entirely inward-looking and by avoiding an over-emphasis on 'situationally determined' explanations which ignore wider influences. It opens up a veritable Pandora's box of treasures for those who will only lift the lid.

In attempting to answer the question of why comparison actually *matters* we have shown, in chapter 3, that the failure to engage in comparative research led, in Britain at least, to a series of partial, and often inaccurate, accounts of how social policies evolved in industrial societies. There was a tendency to fall back upon 'great man' theories of policy development and too ready an assumption that social reforms to house, educate and protect the working man and his dependents were obvious measures taken by any civilized society. The inevitability and sequence of the events growing out of industrialization and urbanization were taken for granted. Social policy analysts with a detailed knowledge of their own country and a superficial familiarity with others were excited by the apparently similar developments taking place, and accepted that a convergence in practice across different societies would eventually result. The emphasis, essentially, was on points of similarity rather than on points of difference.

In this book we have pursued a somewhat different approach arguing that both developing and advanced societies are faced with a series of common problems which require (but do not always attract) solutions. The ways in which these societies have responded to such problems, far from being standardized, have been enormously varied both in administrative detail and in general orientation. The interesting question, for the social scientist, is why there should be such variation in the face of common problems. In earlier chapters we have pointed to what some, although obviously not all, of these problems might be. We have talked not only about the satisfaction of basic human needs such as the need for shelter, food, medical care and some form of income, but also about how to provide for the able-bodied unemployed in societies which place a high value upon the meaning of work.

We have also attempted to answer the question of what factors determine these different responses. A review of the literature, in chapter 4, suggested a wide range of possibilities. These included the degree of centralization of the political system, the ethnic and demographic composition of the population, the size and strength of the working class, the extent of unionization of workers, the 'age' of the welfare system, the nature of the political and economic system, the level of technological development and the role of the military. We concentrated particularly upon two possible determinants: firstly, the 'role of the State' because that subsumed a number of important issues under one broad heading, and secondly, the 'role of religion' because this is an interesting and important area which has largely been ignored in previous work.

Finally, we have considered some of the options facing policy-makers and have looked at the different outcomes which resulted. A central issue concerns the relationship between the world of work and the world of welfare. Chapter 6 looked in some detail at the complex interconnections between the two and at the many dimensions of the work and welfare linkages. Another important area of choice is that between public and private systems of care. We do not imply by this that the balance achieved between the two in any society is necessarily the result of conscious deliberation and planning. Clearly responsibilities for the very different types of public and private welfare system are diverse and the systems have developed accordingly — under the aegis of innumerable agencies and often on an *ad hoc* basis.

In exploring these issues we have concentrated especially upon comparison historically and cross-nationally, at a high level of generalization. This is not, of course, a substitute for more detailed studies of particular aspects of policy at the micro level. Ideally the one approach should be used to complement the other. The macro approach offers broader perspectives and provides context for micro studies, while the micro approach provides facts, information and precision without which the macro approach would be hollow and abstract. The reader must always decide for her/himself which approach is the more appropriate for her/his own purposes. Neither method is inherently superior to the other. There are obviously many other types and levels of comparison than those illustrated here: for example, we can point to useful research which compares different spending patterns of local authority areas in Britain, or the policies of different States in America. Such research has been used recently to examine the effects on the homicide rate of the abolition of the death penalty in some States and its retention in others. Similarly, papers presented in a number of workshops organized by the Social Science Research Council have shown that comparisons between the different regions of the United Kingdom may also offer valuable insights. We are not, therefore, confined simply to comparisons between different countries.

One of the main conclusions to emerge from this development of the comparative perspective in the study of social policy is that the idea of large-scale convergence is not borne out. Although policies may be strongly influenced by many of the factors enumerated above they are not in the unremitting grasp of external forces such as 'technology' or 'ideology'. Within very broad parameters policy-makers exercise choice, it will not be an entirely free choice but one at least which is sufficiently flexible to prevent all industrial societies tumbling headlong into the melting pot of convergence. This element of choice is important and it helps to account for some of the variations in approach and in outcome which we have observed. The fact that choice exists also means what while some nations will wish to accord a high priority to public expenditure on social welfare other nations may not. For all industrialized societies to converge along the same path of change in social policy they have, to some extent, to wish to do so — or as Wilbert Moore put it (in a slightly different context), 'For the world to beat a path to the door of the inventor of a superior mousetrap, it must first be interested in catching mice' (Moore, 1951, p. 182).

Choice in social policy

In rejecting the theories of convergence which have sought to account for and predict long-term changes in industrial societies we do not deny that social policy in some countries has developed along similar paths to that in others. Clearly, there are points at which the similarity of policy response and outcome (for example, in the development of poor laws in pre-industrial Europe) has been very striking and the extent of the overlap has been a phenomenon to be explained. What we have rejected in convergence theories is the notion of inevitability which they embody, the belief that a single 'grand theory' of change in society and social policy is adequate and their failure to take account of variations in practice. On the other hand, the antithesis of this position is equally hard to support with comparative evidence. Obviously Rational Economic Man does not sit behind a desk with a series of clear-cut policy alternatives set out before him and, exercising his free will, choose between them. On the contrary policy-makers everywhere operate within a number of important constraints, whether they are the constraints of history and of precedent, or whether they are economic or political limitations. The outcome is frequently a compromise between the demands of competing interests, although the demands of particular interest groups may consistently predominate. Hence, we may find that social policies for the employable invariably serve the needs of business, employers and certain government agencies rather than those of the claimant him/herself.

The very essence of political debate, however, concerns these questions of choice. If all the features of social policy were indeed determined by technological forces there would be little controversy and almost nothing to argue about. Even the most superficial comparative research — whether it be historical, intra-national or cross-national — indicates that there *are* things to argue about in the making and administration of social policy. We have pointed to some of them, but there are many others. Governments choose, in effect, between residual and institutional models of welfare. By their actions, if not by their rhetoric, they determine whether the

State provides welfare as a last resort or whether it is in the front line in the battle against social need. They determine, too, what proportion of the national welfare effort will be provided through public sources, and what degree of freedom the private market will have in offering an alternative. There is also the choice between universal, comprehensive benefits and selective benefits (or 'positive discrimination') for particular groups in need. Should such benefits be provided at some cost to the consumer or should they be free at the point of receipt? Are benefits in cash preferable to benefits in kind and how should they be financed?

The denial that such choices actually exist has both theoretical and practical implications. As Titmuss argues, the 'post hoc' analysis of social policy as having been 'functionally necessary' in industrializing societies:

> has given rise to deterministic welfare theories and has contributed to the belief that moral problems of choice can be resolved or avoided by technological means and by 'social engineering' answers. . . . The ancient faith, as Berlin has expressed it, in a 'final solution' reappears, with affluence, dressed in technological garments. (1973, p. 272)

One effect of such beliefs would be to justify government non-intervention to relieve social distress on the grounds that technology or the market will solve the problems. The weakness of this position has been demonstrated by a number of writers in recent years, not least by Martin Rein, who observes that:

> Science and technology cannot rescue us from the abiding issues of choice among conflicting but desirable social objectives. Indeed, by increasing wealth, technology and science exacerbate the problem of choice. (1970, p. x)

Whatever scientific and technological aids are employed to assist in the process, actual choices between competing policy alternatives are made by people and not machines. In the same way, social science is limited in the assistance which it can offer. As Rein again points out, although it may supply 'a rational argument for choices made on other grounds; it does not provide rules for choosing' (p. xiv).

One of the dangers of comparative research in social policy, especially where the idea of choice is emphasized, is that the results will be taken as evidence of who does what best. In certain circumstances, where the purpose of the research has been a policy-oriented survey of 'good practice' (for example American cross-national research on public systems of health care), this is clearly legitimate. However, comparative research of the type we have discussed in this book is emphatically not prescriptive. Its aim is to explain rather than to prescribe. The fact that previous comparative teaching not infrequently produced generations of 'little Englanders' who believed that the purpose of cross-national research was to demonstrate that 'British is Best', is one of the problems that we have been attempting to overcome. This is not to say that questions about value and efficacy have no place in the study of social policy, but simply that a distinction should always be maintained between description and prescription. Readers of this book will appreciate that it has been concerned with the former and not the latter. As Heidenheimer et al. point out 'Comparative analysis of policies will not prescribe any ultimately "right" way to balance the extraordinarily difficult choices that are necessary' (1976, p. 281). It can, however, illustrate what some of those choices are; it may, in some circumstances, indicate the magnitude and variety of choice involved and it may also suggest criteria by which different choices could be evaluated.

The importance of theory

Much of the above discussion indicates that one of the persisting concerns in comparative analyses of social policy has been the need to develop theory to guide our studies. As Pinker observes:

> one of the problems associated with the comparative study of social welfare systems stems from the lack of a classificatory framework which would help us to distinguish the key institutional and normative features of different kinds of welfare system from the mass of descriptive data which research is making available for study. (1979, p. 223)

Marxist analysts are probably exempt from this general observation because, in a sense, they begin with theory and move on to empiricism. However, the great majority of non-Marxist studies in social policy, which use comparative data, reverse this process. They begin with careful, and often very detailed, case studies and data-collecting exercises, and only secondly (if at all) do they attempt to place them within a broader theoretical framework. However, this apparent weakness in the study of social policy can be converted into one of its greatest strengths. There are few other areas of study which have such well established empirical foundations. Few, therefore, have the advantage of such good basic materials from which to carve out sound theory. The empirical tradition in the study of social policy (especially in Britain) should not, therefore, be regarded — as it so often is — as a cause for apology but, on the contrary, as a valuable asset. The field of 'social policy and administration' which has, in the past, been regarded as a poor relation amongst its academic peers — sociology, economics and political science — (largely because of its lack of theoretical depth), is due to come of age.

However, some of the most vociferous critics of theory-building in social policy have come from within this field of study itself, and it will be important to reassure them that the exercise is a useful one. A distinguished writer and teacher in social policy recently remarked that our primary concern should be with *how* things work and not *why*. In other words our task, he felt was one of description rather than analysis. Barbara Rodgers, too, warns us to 'be wary of the academics whose major preoccupation is theory-building' (1978, p. 199). There are others who argue that, within this field of study more than any other, we should be concerned, first and foremost, with the relief of social distress, rather than abstract theorizing. While this view may have some validity, it is important to recognize that the two activities are not mutually exclusive and, furthermore, that we can become better at the former by becoming more proficient at the latter.

One way of meeting the criticisms may be by answering the questions 'what is theory?' and 'what is it for?'. The first point to be made is that we are advocating more concerted attempts to develop *some* theory *for* social policy, rather than *a* theory *of* social policy. We are not looking for, and indeed would not expect to find, a single all-embracing theory of social policy which would be applicable in all cases. The kind of theory employed in this book, then, at its simplest and most basic is essentially a means of organizing knowledge. This is an important function because it is a means of preventing what one might call *knowledge slippage.* In othe words, without some rudimentary framework for ordering data, we are in danger of moving from one 'case' to another in social policy, unable to benefit from past experiences and mistakes and unable to contribute to the cumulative growth of learning and understanding. Unless steps are taken to prevent it, knowledge slips down the cracks and crevices between one 'case' and another and — if not lost for ever — it is, at least, underutilized. If one answer to the first question, then, is that theory is a means of organizing knowledge, answers to the second question are somewhat more diverse.

'What is theory for?' The three main attributes of theory in social policy are that it allows us to *generalize,* to *explain* and to *predict.* All three functions are important for purely pragmatic, as well as for more esoteric, reasons. In a field of activity which so intimately affects the welfare of individuals, families and communities, and one to which governments and private interests contribute considerable resources, we need to know how things are as they are and how they might change as a result of different courses of action. Theory allows us to establish correlations between otherwise isolated pieces of knowledge, and enables us to identify regularities. It gives us a sense of what is 'normal' and 'usual'.

The next questions we might consider are 'Are new developments in theory really necessary?' and 'What is wrong with the current state of the art?'. To these we will reply that, although there have been some notable attempts to develop theory, in the study of social policy, these contributions do not go far enough and we must aim to take them further. As many of their authors would readily admit they have, essentially, been concerned with cutting away the undergrowth and we are, only now, beginning to emerge into the clearing. Furthermore, a number of them (and I count myself amongst them) have been concerned not so much with fashioning sound theory in social policy but with analysing 'theories of theories of social policy' (see Pinker, 1971; George and Wilding, 1976; Mishra, 1977; Baker, 1979; Room, 1979; Higgins, 1980). While this is a valuable exercise it is only the first stage in developing coherent and relevant bodies of theoretical knowledge.

One reason why the current state of the art is sometimes regarded as less than satisfactory is that social policy has been, until recently, the magpie of the social sciences. Although it has stolen some glittering methodological trinkets from the nests of sociology, economics and political science we have found that, whilst there have been some real gems in the haul, they have not all necessarily been of use to us. It has become increasingly clear to writers and researchers in the field of social policy that we need to furnish our nests with our own materials. Whilst we may continue to borrow concepts and methods from the other social sciences we must continually aim to modify them in ways which will suit our aims and interests as well as, at the same time, looking for new ways of organizing our data more appropriately.

The final set of questions we must confront are 'what kind of theory do we want?' 'what problems must it resolve?' and 'what issues should it deal with?'. A number of different types of theory in social policy have evolved in recent years. Titmuss, for example, developed his theoretical position around a number of *key concepts*. As Reisman points out, these included:

> value consensus, relevance, avoidance of stigma, a universalist infrastructure of welfare services, social costs and benefits, planned redistribution via selective discrimination, the mixed economy, the failure of the market in welfare matters. (1978, p. 175)

This mixture of concepts, Titmuss felt, must be set within a framework which would involve 'structure, function and role, but also ideology and belief' because, as Reisman observes, Titmuss regarded such a framework as:

> essential to a young subject where theory had tended to lag behind practice. He warned that 'the social scientist without an ideological frame of reference rarely asks good questions'.

Pinker, also, in *The idea of welfare* (1979) is moving towards theory in social policy which is concerned primarily with *concepts*. In this case the concepts of 'egoism' and 'altruism', 'nationalism' and 'internationalism', 'individualism' and 'collectivism'. Furthermore, these concepts are explored within the context of a number of *institutions,* such as 'the family', 'the community' and 'the nation'. He, too, is conscious of the need to develop further the theoretical aspects of the study of social policy and describes it as 'one of the issues which I shall explore in the future' (p. 223).

Hall et al. (1975), on the other hand, draw selectively upon *systems theory* for their conceptual framework in analysing a number of case studies in British social policy. Their emphasis is essentially upon *processes* such as the regulation of demand, and the pursuit of support and legitimacy in policy-making. Another contributor to theoretical analyses of social policy, Ian Gough, as we have already indicated adopts *Marxist political economy* as the theoretical backdrop for his study. It is Marxist, he claims, because it is 'founded on the premises of historical materialism', and it is political economy because it is 'essentially concerned with the economy — the way production is organised — and the political and social institutions and processes of society' (1979, p. 10). Carrier and Kendall (1973; 1977), in contrast, offer an analysis of social policy development which is 'based on the "*phenomenological*" *perspective*' (1973, p. 221). This approach, they argue, is designed to examine ' "how and why welfare states have developed" and "what welfare states have accomplished", by studying the processes through which any body of knowledge comes to be socially established and sustained as reality' (p. 220).

Many of these writers, even at this stage, are probably closer to amassing a body of sound theoretical precepts than their modesty allows them to admit. We can identify an analytical approach which is distinctive, which is not fundamentally derivative, and which applies specifically to the study of social policy. This can perhaps be demonstrated best through the use of a case study. The analysis of 'welfare backlash', to which we referred in the last chapter, offers a good illustration of the contribution which can be made by a comparative and a theoretical approach to explanation in social policy. Consider, for example, the following report:

> In the Australian House of Representatives of 31 May 1979 there was a debate on 'the necessity to restrain welfare abuse and wastage so that those in need receive a more equitable share of the welfare dollar'. Speakers in the debate, initiated by members on the conservative side of the House stressed that they had no objection to *genuinely* needy people receiving benefits but despite that there were disparaging comments about the unemployed and single parents. Regardless of the case that could be made for extremely costly policies such as universal pension payments for those over seventy and universal family allowances, these were not even mentioned in the debate. The conservative speakers were clearly taking an opportunity to doubt the legitimacy of claims made by the unemployed and the poor. . . . The debate stresses that abuse is rampant, that a multitude of people are receiving a variety of benefits to which they are not entitled, that the tax dollar is being 'misappropriated' yet unemployment beneficiaries seem to be getting the blame with no mention of Australia's elaborate and well-organised tax avoidance industry. (Graycar, 1979, p. 20)

A British reader of the above account will observe that the issues raised and the language in which they are discussed are exactly the same as those featuring in House of Commons debates from the early 1970s onwards. The kind of objections which Australian politicians voiced are those, almost verbatim, which British Members of Parliament have recently been raising. Similarly, the American observer will agree that debates in Congress about welfare fraud and abuse have been conducted, almost word for word, along the same lines. Many Western Europeans, too, would recognize the same concerns in their own countries. On the face of it, therefore, it seems little short of astonishing that countries so far apart, and so culturally diverse, should perceive a problem of 'welfare abuse' in the same way, with the same anxiety, at the same time. How do we explain such a phenomenon? Let us begin by examining how different groups of analysts might approach the issue.

Some of the early writers on social welfare, whose contribution we reviewed in chapter 3, would clearly have had difficulty in accounting for the developments described above. 'Social conscience theorists', for example, foresaw the growth of 'a widening and deepening sense of social obligation', cumulative change 'in the direction of greater generosity and wider range' and considered social improvement to be 'irreversible' (Baker, 1979, p. 178). Their conception of human society, therefore, was not one which would allow for any fundamental challenge to the gradual amelioration of social conditions. In particular, it could not account for the international nature of the threat except perhaps in terms of a worldwide 'crisis of conscience' (which would be unsatisfactory as an explanation).

Another group of writers (also discussed in chapter 3) would certainly regard the phenomena we describe as further evidence of convergence in societies and their social policies, around the world. However, this explanation has its limitations too. The debate between those who favour reductions in public expenditure and who see welfare abuse and fraud as a major problem, and those who do not, illustrates — at the very least — that we have not seen the 'end of ideology'. Ideological divisions still exist regarding the legitimacy and the priorities of public welfare. At the same time Harold Wilensky (although sympathetic to 'convergence theory') provides evidence which suggests that complex, industrial societies, which may be similar in some respects, are dissimilar in their experience of 'backlash', and in their responses to it. The 'welfare state', he observes, 'is at once one of the great structural uniformities of modern society and paradoxically one of its most striking diversities' (Wilensky, 1976, p. 9).

The conditions in which attitudes to backlash ferment are frequently different. For example, the superficial similarities between public welfare policies in California before, during and after the passage of Proposition 13 and British policies under a Conservative government proved to be *only* superficial. The level and extent of public service provision, in the two countries, differed significantly, as did the means of financing it. The primary responsibility for such provision lay at the local, State, level in California as opposed to the central government level in Britain. Californian cuts in public expenditure centred upon museums and parks and other recreational facilities, refuse collection, fire and police services, and some educational services while, in Britain, they were directed — in the first instance — at the home help service, services for the elderly and the disabled, residential accommodation and other items of capital expenditure, school meals and personal social services. The expression of anti-welfare attitudes was accomplished through a referendum and an amendment to the State constitution in California, but there was no comparable testing of popular opinion, on these particular issues, in Britain. Finally, California had considerable resources upon which to draw for the continued financing of some services — a situation which was not replicated in Britain. Furthermore, in 1978 the Californian economy was booming and although some public service jobs were lost 500,000 new ones were created. In Britain, meanwhile, those made redundant by public expenditure cuts were added to the growing number of unemployed. Thus, two examples, of 'backlash', which are often compared, when examined more closely prove to be different in a large number of important respects.

There are other variations in the pattern of backlash. Countries which devote considerably varying percentages of their GNP to welfare spending (e.g. Denmark, Switzerland and the United States), according to Wilensky, may have similar experiences of backlash, while countries which spend approximately the same proportion of GNP on welfare may experience different degrees of backlash. Obviously, such comparisons are very crude, but we do have enough reliable data to indicate that it would be too simplistic and misleading to take the apparently widespread phenomenon of 'welfare backlash' as evidence of the inevitable convergence of industrial societies.

A third group of writers — Marxist analysts of social policy —

have looked for, and would claim to have found in the 'welfare backlash' issue, a fundamental flaw in the capitalist heaven. James O'Connor, for example, has argued that the 'welfare crisis' arises, in part, from two 'mutually contradictory functions' which the capitalist State aims to fulfill — those of 'accumulation' (amassing profits) and 'legitimization' (maintaining social harmony) (O'Connor, 1973, p. 6). Gough argues, more specifically, that:

> The cuts in expenditure, especially on the welfare state, here and abroad are evidently related to the unprecedented crisis of the world capitalist economy. . . . The seeds of the current world crisis germinated precisely during the preceding 'long-boom' of the post-war years. This both exhausted the post-war potential for accumulation and growth within the capitalist world and altered the class balance of forces within the advanced countries. (1979, pp. 131–2, 135–6)

While the sophistication and richness of many of O'Connor's and Gough's arguments cannot be denied there remain two basic weaknesses. Firstly, there is the implication that tax revolts and 'welfare backlash' are an inevitable feature of capitalist society — especially capitalist society in decline. For O'Connor the present situation lends further support to Marx's observation that 'tax struggle is the oldest form of class struggle' (1973, p. 203), and that it is both inevitable and predictable, given the contradictions of life in a capitalist society. Related to the notion of inevitability is that of 'determinism'. Gough claims, for example, that 'the capitalist economy has a momentum or dynamic of its own which is . . . basically outside the control of any agent or class' (1979, pp. 39–40). Both of these features of Marxist analysis are unsatisfactory as means of explaining the processes by which change in social policy and social structure actually occur.

Secondly, Marxist writers, whilst espousing the desirability of comparative analysis, have tended to draw upon rather a limited range of examples in reaching their conclusions. We might reasonably argue that there are capitalist societies which do not display evidence of 'crisis' — certainly not to the same extent as those (usually Britain and the United States) discussed by many Marxist writers. Conversely, we might argue that certain non-capitalist societies have experienced some of the same 'crises' which are said to be peculiar to capitalist societies. While Marxist analyses have provided some valuable insights, therefore, there remain these two basic weaknesses in their explanatory framework.

Finally, then, what can a comparative, theoretical analysis of social policy offer which will improve upon, or add to, the three kinds of approach outlined above? As we have already indicated our use of the word 'theory' is meant to refer to a means of systematically organizing knowledge and its primary aim, therefore, is not to develop a coherent, ideological statement about the nature of 'the State' and the role of social policy within it as, for example, Marxist theory would do. Nevertheless, our theoretical approach is based upon the assumption that complex, industrial societies are built around conflicting interests, demands and pressures which are resolved, or modified, through political processes. It is not 'grand theory' but it aims, instead, to establish general guidelines for analysing policy in specific cases. We return, therefore, to our original case study to illustrate how our perspective can be used to isolate some of the key issues in the Australian example of 'backlash', which we cited, and to show how they relate to a number of general principles in social policy.

First of all, the comparative policy analyst would be disinclined to use the language of 'crisis'. The notion implies immediacy, an apparently acute, and possibly final, stage in the breakdown of existing structures and processes. However, comparative — especially historical — evidence indicates that many of the components of the so-called crisis are familiar ones. They reflect long-standing dilemmas and contradictions in the making and administration of social policy in advanced societies, but they do not necessarily mean their downfall. If 'welfare abuse' is regarded as a problem it is not a new problem, but a *newly discovered* one. It is here that the phenomenological approach, which Carrier and Kendall began to develop, can best be utilized. It helps us to see how and why conditions which are regarded as 'normal' and 'acceptable' in one period are not so regarded in another. The unemployed and the poor in Australia, for example, have not suddenly materialized, so we need to ask why — at this point in time — the legitimacy of their claim to public support is being challenged. Historical evidence (see Deacon, 1976; 1978) and cross-national comparisons (see Piven and Cloward, 1972; Heclo, 1974) tend to suggest that punitive attitudes to the unemployed become more prominent as the numbers of unemployed increase. Paradoxically, there tends to be an inverse correlation between the extent of need amongst the poor and unemployed, and political willingness to relieve it. The phenomenological approach, however, helps us to understand that politicians do not necessarily respond to a situation *as it is*, but rather *as they see it*. Furthermore, the way they see it will be determined not only by the objective facts of the situation but also by their calculations of political popularity and electoral gain which might result from their response to it. Phenomenology also helps us to understand and explain what Sinfield (1978) has referred to as 'the social construction of the welfare state'. The way in which problems are defined and presented in social policy tends to reflect the views of powerful groups in society. These are disseminated not only through political debate but also through media reports. Graycar, for example, reports that

> The national newspaper, *The Australian*, can always be relied upon to provide evidence of the media engaging in victim bashing. Its editorial on 12 May 1979 headed 'Time to get out the pruning knife' urged the federal government to take little notice of 'all the beggars beating a path to the Cabinet's door' and argued for cuts in social security expenditure with the claim that 'the tree that is easiest to prune is the one with the most foliage'. (1979, p. 21)

Evidence of the power of the press in shaping perceptions of social problems, in other countries and periods, is also provided by Golding and Middleton (1978) and Deacon (1980). As Sinfield observes 'the more successful the social construction of the welfare state in disguising who really benefits, the less likely we are to accept the need for changes to reduce inequalities' (1978, p. 148). It is important to use our theoretical tools in social policy, therefore, to tease out the factors which determine the 'social construction' of social policies, and to ensure that subjective perceptions are distinguished from objective facts.

Secondly, we can also say, from comparative data (and from utilizing the 'models of welfare' described in chapter 3) that the 'conservative speakers' in the Australian example are behaving in accordance with our expectations. They emphasize 'abuse' and 'wastage' and distinguish between the 'genuinely needy' and other classes of claimant. By implication, the over-70s were felt to be genuinely in need (their case for support was not challenged), while single parents and the unemployed (again, predictably) were not. We would also expect (on the basis of our 'comparative' knowledge) that the claims (probably unsubstantiated and probably exaggerated) about the level of welfare abuse would not be seen as comparable with the tax avoidance issue. The 'models of welfare' which we described earlier enable us to predict that politicians (and other groups) who uphold the ideological values and beliefs of conservatism will tend to regard public systems of welfare with disfavour, especially programmes for the unemployed.

Thirdly, we can identify, in this case study, many of the key concepts and issues in social policy which are discussed elsewhere in this book. These can, perhaps, be classified under four headings, although many of the issues raise questions under each of the four headings. These four are policy choice, legitimacy, work and welfare and the 'social division' of welfare.

Under the heading *policy choice* we can see, in the Australian example, that a number of administrative alternatives were available. The debate in the House of Representatives embodied, on a small scale, many of the conflicts between advocates of *selective,* as opposed to *universalist,* social services. Conservative speakers were advocating *positive discrimination* in favour of 'genuinely needy people' as opposed to universalist policies which would ensure coverage of many individuals whom they did not deem to be needy. However, the conservative speakers also tacitly accepted the desirability of universalist programmes (pensions and family allowances) for certain groups which were implicitly regarded as 'deserving'. In terms of policy choice, there was also the conflict (outlined in our discussion of 'models of welfare') between those who advocated *minimum* levels of provision for 'genuine' cases, and those who supported *optimum* provision in order to achieve wider social goals than mere subsistence. We know, from evidence collected elsewhere, what some of the administrative implications would be of the different policy options, especially those relating to the identification of *need* and *genuineness*.

Associated with the administrative issues of identifying need are the philosophical ones of establishing *desert.* Under our second heading of *legitimacy* we can again identify a number of familiar components in social policy debates. The first of these is the distinction, which is made in the Australian example, between the *deserving* and the *undeserving poor* (which dates back at least as far as the introduction of poor laws in seventeenth-century England). Furthermore, we know from past experience which groups in need are likely to be allocated to which category. In particular, we know that the unemployed are very likely to be classified as 'undeserving' and to be treated accordingly. We know that benefits for them, probably more than any other group, are likely to be parsimonious and *stigmatizing*, and will tend to be the first income benefits to come under attack during periods of cutback. There is also a good deal of comparative data (see Piven and Cloward, 1972; Komisar, 1974) which suggests that another group afforded widespread condemnation, often on moral grounds and those of culpability, are single parents. The Australian example again bears this out.

A second component of the debate, under the heading of legitimacy, which is familiar to us is the argument about *entitlement* and the *proper use of public funds*. While the question of entitlement relates back, to some extent, to issues of need and desert the reference to tax dollars being 'misappropriated' brings in some of the arguments which we discussed in chapter 4 about attitudes to the role of the State. It raises questions about the legitimacy of State intervention, but more specifically it raises issues about the collection and distribution of 'public money', through taxation, and claims upon the public purse. More indirectly, it relates to questions of redistribution, its desirability, and the means by which it should be accomplished. Finally, under this heading, the Australian example raises the question of equity. Issues of equity and equality have been regarded as fundamental in the making and administration of social policy and have been widely discussed (see Weale, 1978).

Thirdly, the position of the unemployed as the main villains of the piece, in the debate, underlines many of the comments we made in chapter 6 about the problematic relationship between *work and welfare*. In particular, it substantiates Mencher's claim (quoted earlier) that 'the focal issue for all economic security policy . . . has been the treatment of the able-bodied or potentially productive individual' (1969, p. xvi). Even if the unemployed themselves do not present problems, and even if they display strong incentives to work, many governments still perceive the unemployed as presenting a threat to social peace and a threat to social norms and values. Here again we can employ the phenomenological perspective to help us understand that, even where the *perception* of a problem may be largely unrelated to the *facts* of the problem, it can be subjective perceptions, rather than objective facts, which dominate political debate and shape policy. Such perceptions can lead to what Cohen (1973) has described as 'moral panics' and to the seeking out of scapegoats as a focus for discontent. The unemployed (as in the Australian case) are frequently cast into this role. As far as the alleged abuse of welfare benefits is concerned we also know, from comparative evidence (see Goodwin, 1972; Feagin, 1975; Deacon, 1976; 1978; 1980), that it is frequently exaggerated. Abuse, when carefully investigated, is rarely 'rampant', as it was claimed to be in the Australian debate, but nevertheless continues to be regarded in many industrial societies as a major problem for social policy.

Finally, the Australian example raises the issue which we have discussed, at some length, about the *social division of welfare*. Graycar, in his account of the Australian debate, notes that although considerable attention was devoted to the alleged abuse of the public welfare system, no mention was made of abuse in the fiscal welfare system of 'Australia's elaborate and well-organised tax avoidance industry' (Graycar, 1970, p. 20). This was despite the fact that it was subsequently announced by the Australian Treasurer that 423 million dollars had been lost in the previous year through tax avoidance (p. 21). Although performing similar functions of income maintenance or supplementation (albeit for different groups of people) the three forms of welfare — public, fiscal and occupational — continue to be regarded by most governments as separate and distinct systems, operating according to different standards and different sets of rules. It is perhaps because of this attitude that analysts of social policy continue to regard the 'social division of welfare' as an important focus of study, when examining the relationship between power, social structure and social policy. As Sinfield has emphasized, the virtue of such an approach is that it allows an examination of the processes of change within social systems, and the interrelationships of their different component parts. Thus:

> By drawing attention to the importance of power and the dynamic effect of changes over time in the political economy of the social division of welfare, one is forced to consider again the relation between welfare and the particular form and structure of the society under study. (Sinfield, 1978, p. 153)

Many of the issues which we have discussed under these four headings, in relation to the Australian example, have a much wider significance for the analysis of social policy. They underline some of the value conflicts and contradictions inherent in the aims of social policy within complex, industrial societies. But more than that, they indicate the way forward for more detailed theoretical explanation in policy studies. Each of the key words and concepts mentioned in the above discussion opens the doors to bodies of theory in social policy — on, for example, stigma, need and desert — and it is by identifying the *key words, concepts* and *issues* in any empirical study that we can proceed most systematically with our comparative analyses. In conclusion, then, it should be clear that theory in social policy must address itself to four sets of questions. These are the *political* and *administrative* questions about policy development and choice, the *philosophical* questions about legitimacy, the *economic* questions about the division of labour and its relationship to the division of welfare, and the *sociological* questions about power, social structure and social policy. It must do so in its own terms, drawing on the considerable wealth of empirical data now available, and refining and developing further the techniques of comparative policy analysis. This is the challenge for the future.

Bibliography

Anderson, Odin (1972), *Health care: can there be equity? The U.S., Sweden and England,* Wiley, New York.

Ashford, Douglas (ed.)(1978), *Comparing public policies: new concepts and methods,* Sage, London.

Bailey, Victor (1977), 'Salvation Army riots, the "Skeleton Army" and legal authority in the provincial town', in A.P. Donajgrodzki (ed.) *Social control in 19th century Britain,* Croom Helm, London.

Baker, John (1979), 'Social conscience and social policy', *Journal of Social Policy,* Vol. 8, Pt 2, April.

Barnett, Malcom J. (1969), *The politics of legislation: the Rent Act, 1957.* Weidenfeld & Nicolson, London.

Bell, Daniel (1960), *The end of ideology,* Free Press, Illinois.

Bernstein, Merton (1973), 'Private pensions in the United States: gambling with retirement security', *Journal of Social Policy,* Vol. 2, Pt 1, Jan.

Blackstone, Tessa (1972), *First schools of the future,* Fabian Society, London.

Blackstone, Tessa (1973), *Education and day care for children in need: the American experience,* Bedford Square Press, London.

Boulding, Kenneth (1967), 'The boundaries of social policy', *Social Work,* Vol. 12, No. 1, Jan.

Bowles, Samuel and Gintis, Herbert (1976), *Schooling in capitalist America,* Basic Books, New York.

Briggs, Asa (1961), 'The welfare State in historical perspective', *European Archives of Sociology,* 11.

Briggs, Asa (1972), 'The history of changing approaches to social welfare', in E.W. Martin (ed.), *Comparative developments in social welfare*, Allen & Unwin, London.

Bruce, Maurice (1972), *The coming of the welfare State*, Batsford, London.

Butterworth, Eric and Holman, Robert (1975), *Social welfare in modern Britain,* Fontana, London.

Cahnman, Werner J. and Schmitt, Carl M. (1979), 'The concept of social policy ("sozialpolitik")', *Journal of Social Policy,* Vol. 8, Pt 1, Jan.

Carrier, John and Kendall, Ian (1973), 'Social policy and social change', *Journal of Social Policy*, Vol. 2, Pt 3, July.

Carrier, John and Kendall, Ian (1977), 'The development of welfare States: the production of plausible accounts', *Journal of Social Policy,* Vol. 6, Pt 3, July.

Castles, Francis and McKinlay, R.D. (1979), 'Public welfare provision, Scandinavia and the sheer futility of the sociological approach to politics', *British Journal of Political Science,* Vol. 9, April.

Chambers, Donald (1975), 'Workmen's compensation in the United States: the effects of fifty years of local control and private enterprise on the administration of a social welfare programme', *Journal of Social Policy,* Vol. 4, Pt 4, Oct.

Chubb, Basil (1963), *The constitution of Ireland,* Institute of Public Administration, Dublin.

Cohen, Stan (1973), *Folk devils and moral panics,* Paladin, London.

Coman, Peter (1977), *Catholics and the welfare State,* Longman, London.

Commission of the European Communities (1977), *The perception of poverty in Europe,* Brussels.

Cutwright, Phillips (1965), 'Political structure, economic development and National Social Security Programs', *American Journal of Sociology*, 70.

Deacon, Alan (1976), *In search of the scrounger*, Bell, London.

Deacon, Alan (1978), 'The scrounging controversy: public attitudes towards the unemployed in contemporary Britain', *Social and Economic Administration,* Vol. 12 No. 2, Summer.

Deacon, Alan (1980), 'Spivs, drones and other scroungers', *New Society,* 28.2.80.

Deakin, Nicholas (1974), 'On some perils of imitation', in Richard Rose (ed.), *Lessons from America,* Macmillan, London.

De Tocqueville, Alexis (1954 edn), *Democracy in America,* Vintage Books, New York.

Domhoff, G.W. (1971), *The higher circles: the governing class in America,* Random House, New York.

Donajgrodzki, A.P. (ed.)(1977), *Social control in 19th century Britain,* Croom Helm, London.

Dore, Ronald (1973), *British factory, Japanese factory,* Allen & Unwin, London.

Doron, Abraham (1978), 'Public assistance in Israel: issues of policy and administration', *Journal of Social Policy*, Vol. 7, Pt 4, Oct.

Durkheim, Emile (1938)(8th edn), *Rules of sociological method,* University of Chicago Press.

Dye, Thomas (1976), *Policy analysis,* University of Alabama Press.

Dye, Thomas (1978), *Understanding public policy,* Prentice Hall, Englewood Cliffs, N.J.

Eckstein, Harry (1958), *The English Health Service,* Harvard University Press, Cambridge, Mass.

Eckstein, Harry and Apter, David E. (1963), *Comparative politics,* Free Press, New York.

Edelman, Murray (1971), *Politics as symbolic action,* Yale University Press, New Haven.

Evans, Harry C. (1926), *The American poor farm and its inmates,* the Loyal Order of Moose, Des Moines, Iowa.

Eyden, Joan (1965), 'The growth and development of the social services and the Welfare State', in David Marsh (ed.), *An introduction to the study of social administration,* Routledge & Kegan Paul, London.

Farley, Desmond (1964), *Social insurance and social assistance in Ireland,* Institute of Public Administration, Dublin.

Feagin, Joe (1975), *Subordinating the poor,* Prentice Hall, Englewood Cliffs, N.J.

Feldman, Elliot J. (1978), 'Comparative public policy: field or method?', *Comparative Politics*, Jan.

Fido, Judith (1977), 'The Charity Organisation Society and social casework in London 1869–1900', in A.P. Donajgrodzki (ed.), *Social control in 19th century Britain,* Croom Helm, London.

Finer, The Hon. Sir Morris (1974), *Report of the Committee on one-parent families,* HMSO, London (Cmnd 5629).

Fraser, Derek (1973), *The evolution of the British welfare State,* Macmillan, London.

Fuerst, J.S. (1974), *Public housing in Europe and America,* Halsted Press, New York.

George, Vic and Wilding, Paul (1976), *Ideology and social welfare,* Routledge & Kegan Paul, London.

Gilbert, Bentley (1966), *The evolution of National Insurance,* Michael Joseph, London.

Gilbert, Bentley (1970), *British social policy, 1914–1939*, Batsford, London.

Ginsburg, Norman (1979), *Class, capital and social policy,* Macmillan, London.

Glennerster, Howard (1975), *Social service budgets and social policy,* Allen & Unwin, London.

Golding, Peter and Middleton, Sue (1978), 'Why is the press so obsessed with welfare scroungers?', *New Society,* 26.10.78.

Goldthorpe, John (1962), 'The development of social policy in England, 1800–1914', *Transactions of the Fifth World Congress of Sociology,* Vol. 4.

Goldthorpe, John (1964), 'Social stratification in industrial society', *Sociological Review, Monograph No. 8*, University of Keele.

Goodwin, Leonard (1972), *Do the poor want to work?*, Brookings Institution, Washington, D.C.

Gough, Ian (1975), 'State expenditure in advanced capitalism', *New Left Review,* Vol. 92, July–Aug.

Gough, Ian (1979), *The political economy of the Welfare State,* Macmillan, London.

Graycar, Adam (1979), 'Backlash, overload and the welfare State', *Australian Quarterly,* Vol. 51, No. 3, Sept.

Gronbjerg, Kirsten; Street, David and Suttles, Gerald D. (1978), *Poverty and social change,* University of Chicago Press.

Hall, Penelope (1957), *The social services of modern England,* (3rd ed.), Routledge & Kegan Paul, London.

Hall, Pheobe; Land, Hilary; Parker, Roy and Webb, Adrian (1975), *Change, choice and conflict in social policy,* Heinemann, London.
Halsey, A.H. (1972), *Educational priority,* HMSO, London.
Handler, Joel (ed.)(1971), *Family law and the poor: essays by Jacobus ten Broek,* Greenwood Publishing Co., Westport, Conn.
Harris, Jose (1972), *Unemployment and politics: a study in English social policy 1886–1914,* Oxford University Press, London.
Hay, J.R. (1975), *The origins of the Liberal welfare reforms, 1906–1914,* Macmillan, London.
Hayward, Jack and Watson, Michael (1975), *Planning, politics and public policy: the British, French and Italian experience,* Cambridge University Press.
Heclo, Hugh (1972), 'Review article: policy analysis', *British Journal of Political Science,* Vol. 2, Jan.
Heclo, Hugh (1974), *Modern social politics in Britain and Sweden,* Yale University Press, New Haven.
Heidenheimer, Arnold (1973), 'The politics of public education, health and welfare in the U.S.A. and Western Europe', *British Journal of Political Science*, Vol. 3, July.
Heidenheimer, Arnold; Heclo, Hugh and Teich Adams, Carolyn (1976), *Comparative public policy: the politics of social choice in Europe and America,* Macmillan, London.
Higgins, Joan (1978a), *The poverty business: Britain and America,* Blackwell, Oxford.
Higgins, Joan (1978b), 'Regulating the poor revisited', *Journal of Social Policy,* Vol. 7, Pt 1, Jan.
Higgins, Joan (1980), 'Social control theories of social policy', *Journal of Social Policy,* Vol. 9, Pt 1, Jan.
Home Office (1969), 'Experiments in social policy and their evaluation', Report of an Anglo-American conference, Ditchley Park, Oxfordshire, October (mimeo; unpublished).
Horowitz, David and Kolodney, David (1974), 'The foundations: charity begins at home', in Pamela Roby (ed.), *The poverty establishment,* Prentice Hall, Englewood Cliffs, N.J.
ILO (1972), *The cost of social security,* ILO, Geneva.
James, Dorothy, B. (1972), *Poverty, politics and change,* Prentice Hall, Englewood Cliffs, N.J.
Jenkins, Shirley (ed.)(1969), *Social security in international perspective*, Columbia University Press, New York.
Kahn, Alfred and Kammerman, Sheila (1975), *Not for the poor alone: European social services,* Temple University Press, Philadelphia.
Kaim-Caudle, Peter (1967), *Social policy in the Irish Republic,* Routledge & Kegan Paul, London.
Kaim-Caudle, Peter (1973), *Comparative social policy and social security: a ten-country study,* Martin Robertson, London.

Katznelson, Ira (1978), 'Considerations on social democracy in the United States', *Comparative politics,* Oct.

Kendall, Ian (1979), *Mothers and babies first?*, the National Maternity Grant Campaign, London.

Kerr, Clark (1962), *Industrialism and industrial man,* Heinemann, London.

King, Anthony (1973), 'Ideas, institutions and the policies of governments: a comparative analysis', *British Journal of Political Science,* Vol. 3, No. 4, Oct.

Komisar, Lucy (1974), *Down and out in the U.S.A,* New Viewpoints Edition, USA.

Lawson, Roger and Reed, Bruce (1975), *Social security in the European Community,* PEP, Chatham House, London.

Lawson, Roger and Stevens, Cindy (1974), 'Housing allowances in West Germany and France', *Journal of Social Policy,* Vol. 3.

Lawson, Roger and Young, Michael (1975), 'Cross-national comparison', in Michael Young (ed.), *Poverty Report, 1975,* Temple Smith, London.

Leaper, R. (1975), 'Subsidiarity and the welfare State', *Social and Economic Administration,* Summer.

Leibfried, Stephan (1978), 'Public assistance in the United States and the Federal Republic of Germany', *Comparative Politics*, Oct.

Leichter, Howard M. (1979), *A comparative approach to policy analysis: health care in four nations,* Cambridge University Press.

Leuchtenburg, William E. (1963), *Franklin D. Roosevelt and the New Deal,* Harper & Row, New York.

Liebow, Eliot (1967), *Tally's corner: a study of street-corner men,* Little, Brown, Boston.

Lipset, S.M. (1963), *Political man,* Anchor Books, New York.

Little, Alan and Smith, George (1971), *Strategies of compensation: a review of educational projects for the disadvantaged in the United States,* OECD, Paris.

Lynes, Tony (1967), *French pensions,* Bell, London.

McKay, David H. (1977), *Housing and race in industrial society: civil rights and urban policy in Britain and the U.S.A,* Croom Helm, London.

Madison, Bernice Q. (1968), *Social welfare in the Soviet Union,* Stanford University Press, California.

Madison, Bernice Q. (1973), 'Soviet income maintenance policy for the 1970s', *Journal of Social Policy,* Vol. 2, No. 2, April.

Mandelker, Daniel (1973), *Housing subsidies in the United States and England,* Bobbs-Merrill, Indianapolis.

Mansergh, N. (1958), *Survey of British Commonwealth affairs: problems of wartime co-operation and post-war change,* Oxford University Press, London.

Marmor, Theodore and Bridges, Amy (1977), *Comparative policy analysis and health planning processes internationally,* Dept. of Health, Education and Welfare, Washington, D.C.

Marsden, Dennis and Duff, Euan (1975), *Workless,* Penguin, Harmondsworth.

Marshall, T.H. (1963), *Sociology at the crossroads,* Heinemann, London.

Marshall, T.H. (1967), *Social Policy* (2nd edn), Hutchinson, London.

Marshall, T.H. (1970), *Social policy* (3rd edn), Hutchinson, London.

Marshall, T.H. (1975), *Social policy* (4th edn), Hutchinson, London.

May, Margaret (1978), 'Violence in the family: an historical perspective', in J.P. Martin (ed.), *Violence and the family*, Wiley, London.

Mencher, Samuel (1967), *Poor law to poverty program*, University of Pittsburgh Press.

Miller, S.M. and Roby, P.N. (1970), *The future of inequality*, Basic Books, New York.

Miller, S.M. (1978), 'The re-capitalisation of capitalism', *Social Policy,* Nov./Dec.

Miller, S.M. (1979), 'Social policy on the defensive in Carter's America', *New Society,* 1.11.79.

Mishra, Ramesh (1973), 'Welfare and industrial man', *Sociological Review*, Vol. 21, No. 4, Nov.

Mishra, Ramesh (1975), 'Marx and welfare', *Sociological Review,* Vol. 23, No. 2, May.

Mishra, Ramesh (1976), 'Convergence theory and social change: the development of welfare in Britain and the Soviet Union', *Comparative Studies in Society and History,* Vol. 18, No. 1, Jan.

Mishra, Ramesh (1977), *Society and social policy,* Macmillan, London.

Moore, Wilbert (1951), *Industrialization and Labor,* Cornell University Press, Ithaca, N.Y.

Nagel, Stuart (1975), *Policy studies in America and elsewhere,* D.C. Heath, Lexington, Mass.

Navarro, Vicente (1977), *Social security and medicine in the USSR: a Marxist critique,* Lexington Books, Lexington, Mass.

O'Connor, James (1973), *The fiscal crisis of the State,* St Martin's Press, New York.

OECD (1976), *Public expenditure on income maintenance programmes,* OECD, Paris.

Osborn, Robert (1970), *Soviet social policies,* Dorsey, Homewood, Illinois.

Pinker, Robert (1971), *Social theory and social policy,* Heinemann, London.

Pinker, Robert (1979), *The idea of welfare*, Heinemann, London.

Piven, Frances Fox and Cloward, Richard (1972), *Regulating the poor,* Tavistock, London.

Piven, Frances Fox and Cloward, Richard (1977), *Poor people's movements: why they succeed and how they fail,* Pantheon, New York.

Podell, Lawrence (1969), *Families on welfare in New York City,* Center for the Study of Urban Problems, New York.

Pryor, Frederick (1968), *Public expenditure in capitalist and communist nations,* Irwin, Homewood, Illinois.

Radcliffe-Browne, A.R. (1952), *Structure and function in primitive society,* Free Press, New York.

Radzinowicz, Sir Leon and King, Joan (1977), *The growth of crime: the international experience*, Basic Books, New York.

Rein, Martin (1970), *Social policy: issues of choice and change,* Random House, New York.

Rein, Martin (1973), 'Work incentives and welfare reform in Britain and the United States', in Bruno Stein and S.M. Miller (eds), *Incentives and planning in social policy: studies in health, education and welfare,* University of Chicago Press.

Rein, Martin and Heclo, Hugh (1973), 'What welfare crisis? A comparison of Britain, Sweden and the United States', *Public interest,* No. 33, Fall.

Reisman, David (1978), *Richard Titmuss: welfare and society,* Heinemann, London.

Rimlinger, Gaston V. (1961), 'The trade union in Soviet social insurance: historical development and present functions', *International Social Security Review,* Vol. 14, No. 3, April.

Rimlinger, Gaston V. (1966), 'Welfare policy and economic development: a comparative historical perspective', *Journal of Economic History,* Vol. 26, No. 4, Dec.

Rimlinger, Gaston V. (1971), *Welfare policy and industrialisation in Europe, America and Russia,* Wiley, New York.

Robson, William A. (1976), *Welfare state and welfare society,* Allen & Unwin, London.

Rodgers, Barbara; Greve, John and Morgan, John (1968), *Comparative social administration,* Allen & Unwin, London.

Rodgers, Barbara (1977), 'Comparative studies in social policy and administration', in Helmut Heisler (ed.), *Foundations in social administration,* Macmillan, London.

Room, Graham (1979), *The sociology of welfare,* Blackwell, Oxford.

Rose, Richard (1974), *Lessons from America,* Macmillan, London.

Rose, Richard (1976), *The dynamics of public policy: a comparative analysis,* Sage, London.

Rossi, Peter and Lyall, Katherine (1976), *Reforming public welfare,* Russell Sage Foundation, New York.

Ryan, Michael (1978), *The organization of Soviet medical care,* Blackwell, Oxford.

Ryan, William (1971), *Blaming the victim,* Orbach & Chambers, London.

Rys, Vladimir (1964), 'The sociology of social security', *Bulletin of the International Social Security Association,* Jan./Feb.

Sanders, William B. (1976), *The sociologist as detective,* Praeger, New York.

Saville, John (1957), 'The welfare State: an historical approach', *New Reasoner,* Vol. 3.

Schwcinitz, Karl de (1943), *England's road to social security,* University of Pennsylvania, Pittsburgh.

Seldon, Arthur (1961), *Agenda for a free society,* Hutchinson, London.

Shanas, Ethel; Townsend, Peter; Wedderburn, Dorothy; Friis, H.; Milhoj, P. and Stehouwer, J. (1967), *Old people in three industrial societies,* Routledge & Kegan Paul, London.

Siegel, Richard and Weinberg, Leonard (1977), *Comparing public policies: United States, Soviet Union and Europe*, Dorsey Press, Illinois.

Sinfield, Adrian (1968), *The long-term unemployed,* OECD, Paris.

Sinfield, Adrian (1978), 'Analyses in the social division of welfare', *Journal of Social Policy,* Vol. 7, Pt 2, April.

Sinfield, Adrian and Sinfield Dorothy (1968), 'Out of work in Syracuse and Shields', in Irwin Deutscher and Elizabeth Thompson (eds), *Among the people: encounters with the poor,* Basic Books, New York.

Smith, Alexander T. (1975), *The comparative policy process,* Clio Press, Santa Barbara.

Social Indicators (1976), US Dept. of Commerce, Washington, D.C.

Social Trends (1979), Central Statistical Office, London.

Stein, Bruno (1976), *Work and welfare in Britain and the United States,* Macmillan, London.

Sugimoto, Teruko (1968), 'The contribution of Buddhism to social work', in Dorothy Dessau (ed.), *Glimpses of social work in Japan*, Social Workers International Club of Japan, Kyoto.

Taira, Koji and Kilby, Peter (1969), 'Differences in social security development in selected countries', *International Social Security Review,* Vol. 22, Spring.

Tawney, R.H. (1966), *Religion and the rise of capitalism,* Penguin, Harmondsworth.

Titmuss, R.M. (1958), *Essays on the Welfare State* (1st edn), Allen & Unwin, London.

Titmuss, R.M. (1965), 'Poverty versus inequality: diagnosis', *Nation*, Vol. 200.

Titmuss, R.M. (1968), *Commitment to welfare,* Allen & Unwin, London.

Titmuss, R.M. (1971), 'Welfare rights, law and discretion', *Political Quarterly,* April/May.

Titmuss, R.M. (1973), *The gift relationship,* Penguin, Harmondsworth.

Titmuss, R.M. (1974), *Social policy,* Allen & Unwin, London.

Titmuss, R.M. (1976), *Essays on the Welfare State* (3rd edn), Allen & Unwin, London.

Townsend, Peter (1970), *The concept of poverty,* Heinemann, London.

Trofimyuk, N.A. (1977), 'Social insurance and the trade unions in the USSR', *International Social Security Review,* Vol. 30, No. 1.

Tussing, A. Dale (1974), 'The dual welfare system', *Society,* Jan./Feb.

Weale, Albert (1978), *Equality and social policy,* Routledge & Kegan Paul, London.

Wedderburn, Dorothy (1965), 'Facts and theories of the Welfare State', *1965 Socialist Register*, Merlin Press, London.

Wendt, Paul (1963), *Housing policy: the search for solutions,* University of California Press, Berkeley.
Whyte, J.H. (1971), *Church and State in modern Ireland 1923–1970*, Gill & Macmillan, Dublin.
Wilensky, Harold (1975), *The welfare state and equality*, University of California Press, Berkeley.
Wilensky, Harold (1976), *The new corporatism, centralization and the welfare state,* Sage, London.
Wilensky, Harold and Lebeaux, Charles (1965), *Industrial society and social welfare,* Free Press, New York.
Woodroofe, Kathleen (1962), *From charity to social work,* Routledge & Kegan Paul, London.
Woodsworth, David (1977), *Social security and national policy,* McGill-Queens University Press, Montreal and London.
Zald, Meyer (1965), *Social welfare institutions,* Wiley, New York.

Index